I0816461

TO:

....

FROM:

....

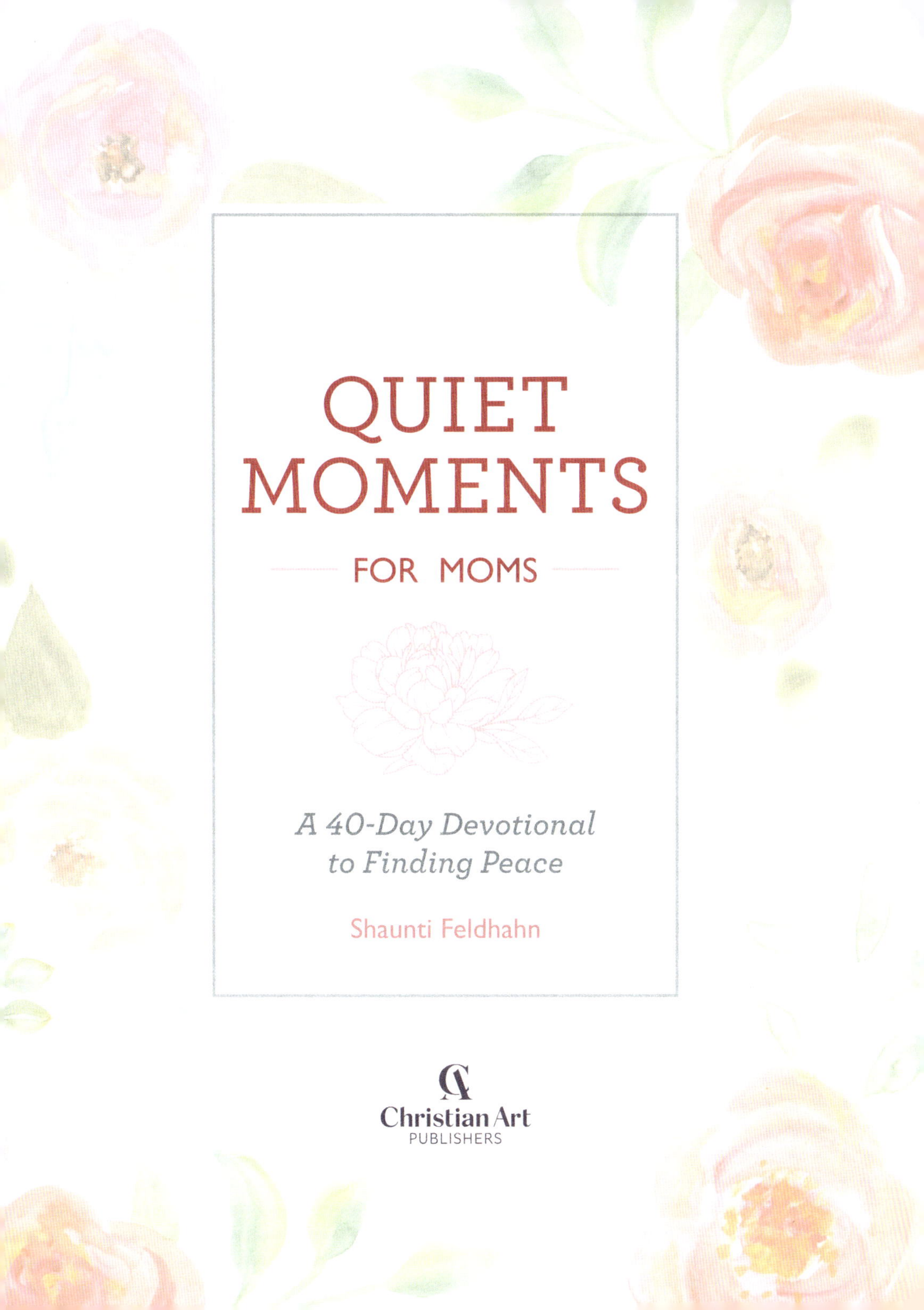

QUIET MOMENTS

FOR MOMS

A 40-Day Devotional to Finding Peace

Shaunti Feldhahn

Christian Art PUBLISHERS

Visit Christian Art Gifts, Inc. at www.christianartgifts.com.

Quiet Moments for Moms: A 40-Day Devotional to Finding Peace

First edition 2025.

Written by Shaunti Feldhahn.

Designed by Christian Art Gifts, Inc.

Cover and interior images used under license from Shutterstock.com

Most Christian Art titles may be purchased at bulk discounts by churches, nonprofits, and corporations. For more information, please email SpecialMarkets@cagifts.com.

ISBN 978-1-63952-900-1

Printed in China

30 29 28 27 26 25
10 9 8 7 6 5 4 3 2 1

Foreword

When I think about the one thing that I want more than anything for my family every single day, I can't think of anything more important than peace. It is priceless. Vital. Desperately needed. And yet, so many of us, including myself, struggle to find peace every day. One of my favorite verses is Philippians 4:7, which says,

And the peace of God, which
transcends all understanding,
will guard your hearts and
your minds in Christ Jesus.

I love this verse because it reminds me that peace is holy and from God, and through prayer and the power of God, we can have peace when it doesn't make sense to the rest of the world. We can have peace in the midst of a heart-breaking diagnosis, a child making questionable decisions, a marital vow being broken, a workplace that seems to be unraveling, and on and on. No matter what we face, we *can* find peace because we *can* always find God. He is with us through it all.

That is precisely why I *love* this devotional. Shaunti pulls readers in with heartfelt stories of real-life struggles, and she shares how she finds peace in the midst of every circumstance. She also offers biblical perspective and even a prayer to help readers focus on the pursuit of peace. And that is the heart of her message—all of us can have peace, but we must *pursue* it every day.

Psalm 34:14 says,

Turn from evil and do good;
seek peace and pursue it.

This devotional leads all of us on a pursuit of peace, and I am so excited to see the blessing that comes to all who are willing to go on this quest. Friends, keep on going after peace with all you have. Peace is a gift from God that He so desperately wants all of us to have every single day, but it takes intentionality. So, go after it. Pursue it. Protect it. Possess it. And, pay it forward. What a blessing it is to have and to give the gift of peace!

Blessed are the peacemakers, for they
will be called children of God.
— Matthew 5:9 —

- Ashley Willis
Author of *31 Verses and Prayers for the Anxious Mind and Heart*
and speaker at MarriageToday

A Personal Note

A friend once told me that to have a child is to have your heart walk around outside your body for the rest of your life. Which is probably why moms have such a need for peace!

Whether our kids are toddlers, teens, or twenty-somethings, a corner of our mind is always attuned to how they are doing. Things can be going smoothly, and we delight in the smiles and laughter—no sickness, no missed deadlines, no broken bones or broken hearts today! Yet even so, our minds jump forward to the "what ifs" of tomorrow.

And that is when things are at their best. What about when there are thunderclouds on the horizon? Or we are already being battered by a storm?

We all need Jesus to speak peace into our worries and troubles. Consider the famous story (Mark 4:35-40, ESV):

> When evening had come, [Jesus] said to them, "Let us go across to the other side." And leaving the crowd, they took him with them in the boat. . . . And a great windstorm arose, and the waves were breaking into the boat, so that the boat was already filling. But [Jesus] was in the stern, asleep on the cushion. And they woke him and said to him, "Teacher, do you not care that we are perishing?" And he awoke and rebuked the wind and said to the sea, "Peace! Be still!" And the wind ceased, and there was a great calm. He said to them, "Why are you so afraid? Have you still no faith?"

Many of Jesus' followers were fishermen. They knew the topography of the Sea of Galilee. They knew it often caused violent, dangerous squalls to arise in an instant. When Jesus directed them to the next ministry location, they knew evening was a crazy time to start crossing open water in a small, probably rickety boat. But they were with Jesus, so they set out.

Maybe they expected that if they were with Jesus, the storms wouldn't come.

Maybe we do too.

But in this life, storms will come. Anxieties and fears will press in. In the midst of turmoil, we may cry, *Jesus, do you not care?!*

Yet Jesus expects His followers to *know* that He cares. To remember that the presence of the gale doesn't mean He has forgotten us.

Like a small child who is carried unafraid through a storm, held tightly by his father's arms, we can have childlike peace amidst the howling wind, thunder, and rain. Simply because He is with us.

That is the profound promise of our Lord. Whether it is a day of great joy or of great pressure, whether He calms the external wind and waves or not, as we trust Him, He *will* calm those in our hearts.

Over the next 40 days, we will be setting out on a journey with Jesus. We will look at what He says about how to have the peace He promises and discover the actions and perspectives He longs to see in every believer. It turns out, many are the same factors that science has found matter most! Imagine that.

Let's be purposeful with our journey, sisters. Regardless of the weather or the waters, let's remember that our hope is Jesus and *He is with us.*

Peace. Be still.

7 Elements of Finding Peace

According to both Scripture and science, these are the key factors that lead to peace—and the actions we must choose in order to receive it. Each devotional will walk through one of these elements as we journey together to *Find Peace*.

- Know God
- Choose Joy
- Release Control
- Demolish Anxiety-Causing Thoughts/Actions
- Create Encouraging Friendships
- Embrace Real Life
- Find Purpose in the Journey

Give all your worries and cares to
God, for he cares about you.
1 Peter 5:7, NLT

Walking Beside Jesus on the Long Journey

We were in a little country church in the mountains of Virginia that Christmas Eve. As we stood for the final hymn, I was looking forward to gathering up the kids, heading back to my parents' cabin, and enjoying a glass of eggnog with my husband, Jeff, while we wrapped the last presents.

Suddenly, in the blink of an eye, something was drastically wrong. Our almost-eleven-year-old son, Luke, stiffened next to me, and then his whole body began to shake. In absolute shock I cried, "He's having a seizure!" and the church erupted.

The next terrifying hours were a blur—the minutes our son was without oxygen during a massive grand mal seizure; the equally scary "postictal" state of being semiconscious and unresponsive; the long race along dark rural roads to the nearest hospital, which was much too far away. It was the longest two hours of my life.

Learning that Luke had epilepsy was the beginning of a long journey, one that seemed even longer once we discovered that medication would control his bodily seizures but not the spikes in his brain. Our straight-A student was transformed into someone who had to work extremely hard just to listen, read, and learn. The same medications that slowed down his brain's dangerous electrical activity also slowed his processing speed and ability to follow group conversations. Suddenly, our friendly, class-clown son had extreme difficulty making friends.

I found myself constantly worrying about him. Each time the school called, my heart caught in my chest. Did he have a seizure? Each time I asked, "Who did you sit with at lunch?" and he answered, "No one," I died a little inside. Luke was generally strong about his new challenges, but in those moments when the dam broke and tears leaked down his cheeks because he couldn't comprehend the page he just read, my heart broke for him. My mind reeled with worries about his future.

You may know that feeling. Your long journey of worry is probably different, but in my research over the years, it is rare to find a mom whose mind doesn't occasionally travel down trails of anxiety or fear. Maybe your worry isn't medical, but about living in an unsafe neighborhood, the effects of an unwanted divorce, the daily bullying in middle school, or the pressure of grades in high school. That awareness is always there in the back of our minds.

A year or two into our epilepsy journey, I finally realized: The reason we worry is that we haven't yet grasped that the awesome God who created the heavens truly cares for us down here on earth. That is why Jesus came, after all. He is suffering with us in the moments of terror or heartbreak. He rejoices in the victories. When a boy who feels stupid and a mom whose heart quakes sit on the couch with tears running down their cheeks, God wraps His arms around both of them to bring peace.

Jesus promises to give us peace in the long journey if we will only take our anxieties and fears and give them to Him. The real journey is to walk alongside Him on the path He has for us—wherever it leads—knowing that it is set before us by One who loves us more than we can comprehend.

In dark moments, we somehow believe that if God really loved us and our kids, He wouldn't let bad things happen. And yet Jesus tells us directly that in this world we will have trouble, but to take heart because He has overcome the world. There will be a day when this world and all its troubles are swept away. And what will be left is the same great God who loved us all along.

Prayer

Jesus, I give You the anxiety I'm experiencing over this hard thing that has come into my life. I wasn't expecting it, and I don't want it. Yet You promise to walk with me and care for me on the journey. I choose to put my focus on that fact and receive Your peace. I give You this situation knowing that You love me more than I can comprehend and that I can cast all my cares on You. Thank You for being my strength. I trust You, Lord. Amen.

Reflect

What is your long journey? Thinking back over the last few weeks and months, what are three signs that God is caring for you on your journey? How might keeping those things in mind change how you experience the next few months of the path?

NOTES

Day 2

May the God of hope fill you with all joy and peace as you trust in him, so that you may overflow with hope by the power of the Holy Spirit.
Romans 15:13

Choosing a Heart of Joy

Marie could not recall hearing her parents ever say anything positive to her when she was a child. She never heard the words, "I love you." Instead, her parents seemed to actively highlight her faults. Marie distinctly remembers the moment she stepped into the living room in a gorgeous prom dress, and her dad looked up at her and said, "You look beautiful . . . like a *battleship*."

This treatment deeply impacted Marie's heart. She knew her parents had difficulty expressing emotion—her father had been orphaned young and her mother was an extreme introvert—but still, why would any parent act this way? She wrestled with bitterness and anger.

Years passed, and she had young children of her own when she realized that all these negative emotions were beginning to spill over into how she was treating her precious little ones. Feeling insecure in herself, she would easily snap at her children, then dissolve into tears when she saw their hurt faces. She desperately wanted to break the cycle but didn't know how.

Have you ever been there? Anyone who has experienced a deep heart wound knows how easily anger or hurt can settle in our bones. And most of us know that inner turmoil will impact our external choices as moms in some way unless we break the cycle.

Her husband advised Marie, "This has eaten at you for too long. Take time off work, fly home, and ask your parents about this. Even if you get no answers, at least you'll have asked."

Marie took his advice, and soon she found herself sitting across the kitchen table from her mother. With no animosity or blame, she asked, "Mom, why did you and dad choose to raise me the way you did?"

Since it was a deliberately open-ended question, she expected her mother to say, "What do you mean?" Instead, she was stunned by what she heard.

"From the youngest ages, you always learned things so quickly," her mother said. "You scared us. All your cousins had become such horrible brats because they were not only smart, but also coddled and pampered. We were worried that you would grow up and think you were better than everyone else. We didn't want that for you."

Although Marie strongly disagreed with their actions, she suddenly recognized that her parents chose to put her down not because they didn't see her as special, but because they worried she would think she was *too* special. They wanted her to be humble instead of arrogant. And yes, they succeeded in raising a woman who never thought she was better than anyone else. But she also never felt good enough, loved, or valuable. Now, she was at risk of passing those feelings along to her own children instead of passing along a sense of gratitude, worth, and delight in life.

Armed with this new knowledge, Marie saw how to break the cycle: She had to choose to live out an alternative to both the negative feelings about herself and the negative feelings about her parents. She had to choose a heart of joy.

While she is certainly still impacted by the way she was raised, Marie now chooses to see the well-intentioned heart behind her parents' damaging actions. If anger wells up, she chooses forgiveness and even gratitude for those things they did well. Most importantly, she chooses to raise her kids in a completely different way. She works hard to both teach humility *and* affirm her children's God-given uniqueness and giftedness. Each time she takes these steps, turmoil is replaced by peace.

It isn't always easy. But she is giving her children a gift that will last for generations, and we can too: demonstrating how to choose joy.

Prayer

Heavenly Father, protect my kids from being wounded by me while You heal my heart. Whenever I doubt that I am beautifully made, show me how You see me. Help me to focus on gratitude and forgiveness. As my heart swells with joy, may it spill over to my children, letting them know they are precious to You and to me. May our home be one that is always marked by Your joy. Amen.

What is a wound that has hit your heart—one that might hamper how you interact with your children? Perhaps you felt like the kid nobody liked, so you're overly sensitive to how your children are treated. Or your mom was derisive, so you snap at the slightest sign of disrespect from your child. Ask God to show you how to choose joy and break that cycle by how you respond in the future. Write down at least one thing you can do differently.

NOTES

Day 3

I sought the Lord, and he answered me;
he delivered me from all my fears.
Psalm 34:4

What Are You Searching For?

In the last weeks before we moved my oldest child into her dorm at an urban college, I found myself getting misty-eyed at the oddest times. My daughter had taken to patting me on the shoulder and saying, "That's okay, Mom, you're fragile." I was. I still am. But I was excited about her new adventure, too. I was eager to see what God had in store.

Unfortunately, that still didn't translate to completely sane thinking.

The day after we dropped her off, I continuously checked the tracking app she still had on her phone. (In lieu of attaching a beacon to her head, this seemed like the next best thing.) "Oh, look, she's at lunch!" "Oh, look, she must be at that sorority rush meeting!" "Oh, look, she's walking across campus; she must be going to that international dining hall."

It was a tiny little glimpse of a girl I already missed so much it hurt.

Jeff humored my slightly obsessive stalking. I told him it made me feel better knowing where our daughter was and guessing what she might be doing.

Late that night in bed I checked the app one more time. Her little dot appeared right outside an unfamiliar dorm.

"Cool, she must be at a party, making new friends."

But in the next moment it was moving at great speed—away from campus to a large condo complex across town! At 11 p.m.!

Suddenly I was on high alert, my thoughts whirring. How could she be in a car? Very few freshmen had one. I knew parties at this massive public university would be a stark wake-up call from her low-key friends at her small, Christian high school. She'd had no experience extricating herself from a situation where someone was drinking and driving.

Before I could stop them, my thoughts flitted down scarier paths: Someone could have thrown her into a car!

I had to know. My heart beating fast, I pulled up a maps app and located the looming building in the midst of the condo complex. I zoomed in.

It was a Target.

I didn't know whether to laugh or feel ashamed of myself. I shakily texted her a falsely cheery greeting.

"How are you enjoying your first night at school? I'm still up if you want to call."

Two minutes later, the phone rang.

"Hey, Mom! Guess what? It's college night at Target! They even had a shuttle; I'm here with all the girls from my hall!"

As I hung up the phone, I glanced sideways at Jeff. Trying not to laugh, he said, "We need to talk about this."

Obviously, I was not handling things well. I needed to start weaning myself from the app. But more importantly, I realized I was seeking comfort and reassurance in entirely the wrong place. I wanted to know where my daughter was without being willing to rest in the fact that God knew. I scrambled for information to make me feel better instead of trusting her to God's care. A care that wouldn't change whether she was in my home or in her dorm or shopping at Target at 11 p.m.

Continually placing our children into the care of our Heavenly Father is the only way to peace. There are so many things in this world that can terrify us (and we moms can come up with some pretty spectacular scenarios, am I right?). But when we're fearful, we need to be like the psalmist who "sought for the Lord." Not an app. Not more information. Not the reassurance of a phone call.

There will always be one more phone call needed. One more situation. One more worry. The only permanent, unshakable peace is found in Him.

Prayer

Jesus, Prince of Peace, thank You that You know my tendency to worry, and You still have infinite patience with me. Lord, forgive me for seeking comfort and reassurance in more information or greater control rather than trusting in You. Give me the strength to let go. Thank You for the joy of raising children through each season of life. I pray that in moments of fear, You will remind me to search for You. I know You are trustworthy; please help me to live that way! Amen.

Reflect

In what areas have you found yourself trying to get answers or control things in order to feel safe and secure? The next time you find yourself doing that, what can you do that will help you trust the Lord instead?

NOTES

Day 4

We demolish arguments and every pretension that sets itself up against the knowledge of God, and we take captive every thought to make it obedient to Christ.
2 Corinthians 10:5

Room 316

Charlotte's five-year-old son was battling a steadily worsening case of pneumonia. His lung function was bad, and he had been sick for two weeks, so there was an element of relief when the doctor looked at her and said it was time to check him into Children's Hospital. The worry was heavy, and her thoughts spiraled with scary scenarios. She was glad to be in a place where the professionals could help shoulder her burden.

The nurses were hooking up her little boy, Henry, to IVs and getting him x-rayed when Charlotte learned what room they'd be in: room 316. Her husband looked at her and said, "That's significant, don't you think?" 316. John 3:16.

"Yeah," she tried to smile. It never hurts to have the most popular Bible verse of all time as your room number.

Now, if you've spent any time at a children's hospital, you know that they are remarkable places—equal parts wonderful and devastating. You can just as easily meet a clown with a golden retriever walking down the hallway as a father, collapsed on the floor, sobbing. Relief and laughter share thin walls with despair and fear.

That first night, Charlotte stood outside Henry's room, raw and anxious from seeing so much real life under one roof. As she fought back swirling thoughts, she could only pray, "God, my son is in that room." And he brought her back to 3:16. He whispered, "Yes, I know. My Son is in that room too."

Most of us know John 3:16 by heart: "For God so loved the world that he gave his one and only Son, that whoever believes in him shall not perish but have eternal life." But have we really stopped to think about the fact that God sent His *Son* so that we may have a personal, thriving, close, real relationship with Him? Most of us would be willing to give our own lives to save our child. How much infinitely harder would it be to allow our child to sacrifice himself or herself for others? And yet God did exactly that. There is no greater demonstration of how intensely our God loves us and how *tangibly* He is with us always.

Because God has so purposefully demonstrated this, there's something specific He asks us to do when we find ourselves overtaken by emotion, or difficult circumstances, or worry, or stress. Paul says in 2 Corinthians that we must "take captive every thought to make it obedient to Christ." Back when Paul was writing this, prisoners were often chained to a guard. On several occasions, Paul was literally connected to a Roman soldier around the clock. He was captive to whoever was attached to the other end of those chains.

Friends, to whom or what are we tethered? God does not want us shackled to our fears. He calls us to freedom. And hope. And *peace*. We get there by grabbing the thoughts and worries of our heart that are trying to spiral out of control and making them captive to *Christ*.

Can't you see it now? Picture yourself linked closely to Jesus, a hairbreadth away, rather than chained to anxiety or, like Charlotte, frozen in fear outside her son's hospital room. When you think the equivalent of, "O God, my son is in that room," remember: *My Son is in that room too.*

Let's connect to the Son of God—who loves us, is for us, and will sustain us—by a bond that cannot break. We are not captive to our oppressor. We are captive to our *Savior.* And He is always, always with us.

Prayer

God, the battle against worry and fear feels as if it is always ongoing. The possible negative outcomes seem so plausible. Yet I know that You are with me. I know that when I redirect my focus toward You and Your presence, those thoughts are demolished and worry goes away. Help me take my fearful thoughts captive. Help me to remember that though my child is in this difficult situation, Your Son is right there also. Amen.

Do you face regular concerns about your children or your life over things large and small? When your thoughts and worries are beginning to spiral, how can you recognize it and take those thoughts captive? In the space below, write down an example of an anxious situation that happened recently and what it would have looked like to make those thoughts captive to Christ instead.

NOTES

Day 5

Let us think of ways to motivate one another to acts of love and good works. And let us not neglect our meeting together, as some people do, but encourage one another.
Hebrews 10:24–25, NLT

Too Busy for Bible Study

When Olivia's two sons were young, she loved giving them the chance to do all sorts of activities—even if it was a bit exhausting. You want to do Little League Football *and* Soccer with your friends? Great! But you also need piano lessons. Oh, your classmates are doing Cub Scouts? That makes sense too. And we can't forget church activities . . .

Olivia's husband had become involved in a men's Bible study, and he started encouraging her to join one for women. Her response? "When in the world would I be able to do *that*?"

While it sounded good in theory, she didn't have that sort of time. After all, in addition to the meeting, there would be weekly reading and homework.

Doing that at some point will be wonderful, she thought wistfully. *But it'll have to wait until the boys are older.*

One day Olivia was telling an older, wiser friend about this conversation with her husband and was getting a bit agitated. Of *course* she would love to do a Bible study! But clearly her husband didn't understand all the demands on her time—especially with so many things she had to do for their boys!

Her friend gently held up a hand. "Do you?"

Bemused, Olivia stared at her friend. What? Of course she did!

Wait. Did she?

Olivia saw just how much she had given in to a sneaky but dangerous pattern. She was so determined that her boys not miss out on anything that *she* was missing out on something much more important. She was putting her boys' social calendar ahead of her relationship with the Lord. And that meant this situation with her children had become an idol.

Oh, that's bad, she thought, wincing ruefully. *There's a commandment about that!*

Olivia sat down with her husband that night. They jointly decided that each child would be limited to choosing one activity per season. She looked into finding a Bible study group that met during the boys' school hours. She connected with a small group of believers in every season of life—some with older kids, some with young kids, and some with no children at all. But they were all women who wanted to know more about Jesus and were making it a priority to meet and support each other.

Olivia discovered that as she put her relationship with the Lord first, time seemed to expand. Each week she was able to do her weekly Bible study reading and homework and still get her boys to their chosen activities, to piano lessons (her choice for them!), and to the church events she and her husband prioritized as a family. Her faith and her relationship with Christ began to grow in ways she could not have imagined.

She also found an incredible community of women to do life with. They were transparent with each other, sharing the good, the bad, and the ugly. They mentored each other, prayed for each other, and spoke into each other's lives. Olivia saw that running around and putting her children's activities first had not really accomplished much of importance. But her time in this Bible study was life changing—for her and, as a result, her whole family.

Sisters, we are created for community. When we try to do life on our own—when we prioritize our children over our relationship with the Lord, our marriage, or our friends—we often become misguided in our priorities and focus. Let us not miss out on what the Lord wants to teach us. Let's be sure we don't forfeit the peace and blessing He so desperately wants us to receive.

Prayer

Heavenly Father, thank You for drawing me to You. Please gently show me where I have created idols and have put other things before growing in my relationship with You. Forgive me, Lord. Even though my intentions were good, I was wrong. Please give me friends who will speak Your truth into my soul. Help me to also share Your truths and encouragement with them. Lord, when my schedule feels cluttered, remind me that You created me to worship You. Amen.

Reflect

Have you found a community of women to help you grow in your relationship with the Lord? If you have, take a moment to thank God for them and write down a few of the ways that your faith has grown through them. If you haven't, what is keeping you from doing so? Are there any misplaced priorities that you need to acknowledge? Other reasons? What changes could you make that would allow you to connect in this way?

NOTES

Day 6

For if the willingness is there, the gift is acceptable according to what one has, not according to what one does not have.
2 Corinthians 8:12

Step Out of the Comparison Trap

Vicky's night wasn't going according to plan.

The next day was St. Patrick's Day. It was also the day her first-grade son was due to turn in his "Leprechaun Trap" school project. Gabe had been working on it for days with unusual diligence.

The year before, leprechauns had snuck into Gabe's classroom, leaving chocolate coins, messed-up toys, and even—to his glorious surprise—green urine in the toilets. Gabe couldn't wait to see how his trap worked. Vicky couldn't wait to find out which overzealous moms had volunteered to sneak into school at 5 a.m. to arrange everything.

But that night, as they were praying before bed, Gabe prayed they would catch a leprechaun in their house the next morning. He clearly couldn't wait to see the chocolate coins in the kitchen and green urine in the toilets.

"Oh, wait, honey," Vicky said, smiling. "You're building a trap for school. Leprechauns don't come to our house." After a busy day at work with the kitchen still a mess from dinner and three other kids to put to bed, she had no intention of running to the store at 9:30 p.m. for chocolate coins and green food coloring. And who in the world wants to mess up their house *on purpose?*

Gabe stared at her. “What?” he asked. “What do you mean?”

Vicky calmly repeated, “The leprechauns only come to your school, not our home. This was an assignment from your *teacher.*”

Gabe was clearly very upset. “Well, that was a big, old waste of TIME!”

Vicky felt terrible—and angry. He had been working so hard and would now feel his hard work made no difference. It also felt like yet another mom failure, not living up to the expectations set by other more creative and, she assumed, *less busy* moms.

The comparison trap can create a lack of peace in an instant, can’t it, ladies? There’s no end to the places we can go to see someone doing our job bigger, better, flashier . . . and with green food coloring, no less. Just take a look at the ideas on Pinterest. You can even find ideas for an apologies-in-advance goody bag for the airplane—complete with earplugs and some cash for a drink—for when you’re traveling with babies.

I’ve never been good at crafts or holiday goodies, even though I sure wish I was. It is easy to feel like everyone else is doing a better job in this department. Or even to roll my eyes at their “overzealousness.” I hear stories like Vicky’s and think, *Can we all just agree to lower the bar and give busy moms a break?!*

But then I think: My teenage daughter loves this kind of stuff. She volunteered for the prom committee and spent hours creating complicated, beautiful, backlit table centerpieces. It brought her joy. When she is a mom, she will probably *love* to create class goody bags and sneak in green food coloring on St. Patrick’s Day.

If she genuinely gets pleasure from using her creativity and gifts to decorate, celebrate, and bless others, should I deny (or make fun of) the things she's doing? What about other moms? Maybe, just maybe, they aren't "raising the bar" but are simply using their gifts to bless their little corner of the world. Maybe other non-crafty moms like me can accept those gifts, use our own gifts in other areas, and stop feeling "less than" simply because we don't enjoy the same things.

So much of our mom guilt comes because we feel we "should" be like someone else. But like we tell our kids, we're all created different! As we embrace the design and the life God has for us, peace will come. What He has gifted us with is what He asks us to bring to Him.

Prayer

Lord, help me to embrace the life and the gifts You've given me, and set aside comparisons to others You have created differently. In those moments when I feel "less than," speak to my heart and remind me that You see me as Your special creation. Forgive me for being judgmental of others. Help me to see how to apply my unique gifts to parent my children in the way they need, and to bring those gifts to bless others, too. Amen.

In what way am I feeling like I "should" be like someone else? Is that pressure from God—in other words, is it something He wants me to handle differently? Or is that pressure from me? What is the gift that God has given *me* as a mom that I can celebrate?

NOTES

Day 7

We rejoice in our sufferings, knowing that suffering produces endurance, and endurance produces character, and character produces hope.

Romans 5:3–4, ESV

Strengthening Your Left Hand

It had been a hard day for our seventh-grade son. Many days were. As Luke adjusted to living with epilepsy, his brain continued to have spikes. The medicine that prevented bodily seizures also slowed down his processing speed. Subjects that used to come easily were now huge challenges. He had to learn to read again. To learn on his own what other kids learned in class. To keep his motivation up while working twice as hard for worse grades, often wrestling through simple homework long after others were done for the day.

He rarely complained. But there were moments when the dam broke. When he felt stupid. When the long road in front of him hurt his heart. And his tears hurt ours.

On this particular day, I felt so helpless to know how to encourage him. But then Jeff put his arm around our son's shaking shoulders and said, "Bud, do you remember that movie we saw last week, *Cinderella Man*?"

That movie tells the story of real-life boxer James J. Braddock, who lived during the Great Depression. Boxing allowed him to put food on the table. In the ring, he wasn't as effective with his left hand, but he was a powerhouse with his right. Then, tragedy: He broke his right hand. His career was over. He was now competing with thousands of other desperate men for very few day laborer jobs. His family was going hungry. So he hid the fact that his right hand was broken to get steady work at the docks. It was excruciating and exhausting, but each day he would grit his teeth and do most of the work one-handed.

Long after his broken right hand had healed, his old manager approached him to take part in a token fight. Everyone knew he had no chance, but it was a paycheck, so Braddock accepted—and was as shocked as everyone else when he easily won. All those excruciating months of work at the docks had unexpectedly made his "weaker" left hand very strong. It had made him into a champion.

Jeff told our son, "Buddy, that is like what you are going through. These hard things are strengthening you in ways you can't imagine right now. You are having to face things that most people will never face. You are holding up under a burden that would crumble most kids. But you know what? Other kids have their own burdens that you will never have to face. Everyone has something. But that is what God uses to build our character. This . . . this is building your left hand."

When a child is in pain, it is easy to dwell on the "broken right hand." Oh, how we want to spare them the hardship and the tears. Braddock would never have chosen the pain he walked through, just as we would never choose to experience ours or allow our kids to experience theirs. And yet God is wiser than we are. Braddock's story gives us a glimpse of why God tells us to "rejoice in our sufferings." Those hard times we would never have chosen will produce endurance, character, and a hope that we would never trade.

Two and a half years after that conversation, Jeff and I had tears streaking our cheeks for a different reason. At the year-end awards ceremony, Luke was called onstage for not one but two academic medals. Medals he earned not really that year, but during those hard months and years before. Those months when he had stayed inside working so hard, trying to figure out how to learn things again, and not losing hope while he did it—strengthening his left hand.

Prayer

Lord, I confess I've been far from rejoicing in the trials that I bear each day. I've been far from rejoicing in the trials that impact my children. Today, I choose a new path. I choose to trust that as we endure trials, You will use them. You will grow us in endurance and in character. And we can persevere because hope is being produced. Today, I choose to trust You and say that I am eager to see how You will use these trials. Amen.

Reflect

Think back. Have you seen times of weakness in your life or your child's that you now see God was using in some way to build endurance, character, and hope? Consider: What trials are you or your child enduring right now? In some period down the road, how might God use them? Write that thought down and come back and refer to it when things get hard.

NOTES

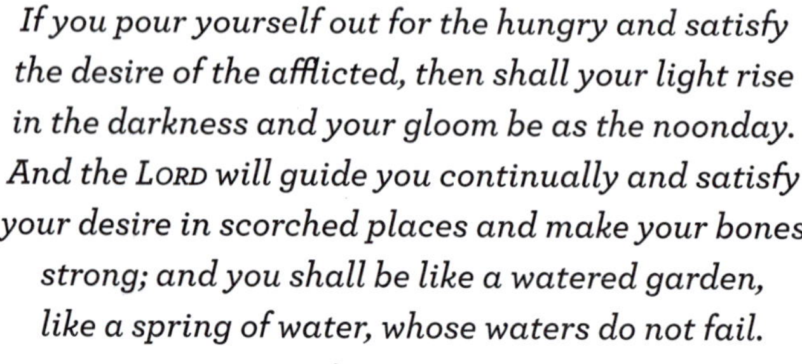

If you pour yourself out for the hungry and satisfy the desire of the afflicted, then shall your light rise in the darkness and your gloom be as the noonday. And the Lord will guide you continually and satisfy your desire in scorched places and make your bones strong; and you shall be like a watered garden, like a spring of water, whose waters do not fail.

Isaiah 58:10–11, ESV

Loud Time with the Lord

Emily sat in her armchair, curled up with her Bible, a cup of coffee balanced precariously on her knee and a peaceful smile on her face. She couldn't have gotten up if she tried; she was surrounded by a slew of young children, a pile of toys, and the dog.

He's looking at me with angry eyes!

Well, she stole my imaginary sword!

Who cares? It's imaginary!

Then give it back! Mooooooom!

Waaaaaaaa!

Woof!

It wasn't that long ago that Emily was flat-out overwhelmed over her day-to-day responsibilities. The noise rattled the windows, she was constantly refereeing squabbles, and she desperately wanted a nap—and that was all before the breakfast dishes reached the sink.

With three kids under age five and a supportive but busy husband, she woke up before the sun and hit the pillow very late at night, only to be up a few hours later to feed the baby. She was grateful but bleary-eyed.

One Sunday after church, Emily bumped into her pastor. When he asked how things were going, she was honest. She was running on empty. And with her young kids, the never-ending sicknesses, the new baby, and very little sleep, she had no ability to fill her tank with a private worship time with God.

Her pastor smiled. "Emily, your whole life right now is worship. In this season you are like a drink offering poured out before the Lord. What you're doing matters, and God sees it. He sees you. He accepts you. He loves you right where you are in the middle of the chaos."

Emily had tears in her eyes. In the midst of this busy, frenetic season—the hours spent worrying and fretting and literally sweating her way through the day—her heart's desire was to connect with the God of peace. She realized she had been waiting for the perfect quiet moment to worship Him. But there was not going to be the "perfect" quiet time in this season!

Emily's pastor encouraged her to change her perspective—to set aside the idea of a quiet time and instead commit to having some "loud time" with the Lord every day. Her children could sit and play at her feet while she read the Bible. She could tell them she would be right here, but that she needed time with God. Let them see her faithfully digging into the Word, her pastor said. Let them see her praying.

Most of all, her pastor encouraged her not to get frustrated or feel like a failure when she was interrupted to fix a Lego creation, change a diaper, or settle a dispute.

The Lord sees you, and your whole life is worship.

Ladies, can we take a collective sigh of relief as we release the burden of creating the perfect worship environment to connect with God? Our lives will never be interruption-free, especially when young children are circling our feet or when things are so busy at work we don't know which end is up. God knows what life is like. There will be seasons of quiet and space. And there will be seasons of noise, and crying, and laughter, and little feet running the halls. God sees us in all of it. He loves us in our chaos just as we love our little people in theirs—and far more.

God promises that as we pour ourselves out in this way, He *will* strengthen us and make us like a vibrant garden; one rich from being watered and cultivated by the Prince of Peace; one rich enough to endlessly pour out to others what He is pouring into us.

Prayer

Lord, I want my spirit to long for You, yet I confess that my best intentions are sometimes hijacked by chaos. And, if I'm honest, sometimes set aside in favor of other priorities. Lord, help me to connect with You whenever and wherever You call to me. Help me to turn my thoughts to You even in the midst of the noise and listen for Your voice. And help me to hear and follow You always. Amen.

Reflect

If a daily "quiet time" with the Lord is impossible in your current season, what would it look like for you to have a "loud time" with Him? Write down several ideas. Then, implement them whenever you might otherwise have trouble connecting with God that day.

NOTES

Day 9

But the fruit of the Spirit is love, joy, peace . . .
Galatians 5:22

Did You Learn How to Love?

Five years ago our closest friends—our kids' godparents—received news that would shatter their world. Although barely over the age of 50, the couple, whom I will call Aaron and Lara, noticed that Aaron had been having weird memory issues. After months of testing, the neuropsychologist gravely said, "We believe it's early-onset Alzheimer's. And I'm afraid there is no cure."

The doctor explained to our stunned friends how the disease progressively affects the brain, ending with, "If I were you, I would get your affairs in order. I'm so sorry."

Knowing that God is the God of the impossible, Aaron and his wife Lara began an intense search for help and hope. They went to many meetings to pray for healing, joined a support group that researched all forms of dementia, transformed their diet, exercised daily, and added powerful supplements and prescriptions to Aaron's routine.

Yet the disease progressed. They had to give up their family business and saw friends drift away. We no longer have high-energy, hilarious game nights listening to Aaron's comedic interpretations. He struggles to carry on a conversation, to remember how to take dishes to the sink. Lara now carries the entire burden of providing for and encouraging the family. They continue to pray for healing. But right now, they are walking through a very, very hard valley.

Yet Lara and Aaron's faith has turned into something that shines like gold. They have lost an entire way of life, but both have a peace that passes all understanding. A peace at which Jeff and I can only marvel. And it is not because they are *trying* to have peace, but because they are trying to be people of love.

As Lara told me, "We all want logical answers and peace in life. But when you look at the fruits of the Spirit, love and joy are listed before peace. I've heard it said that in heaven, God will hug us and ask us: 'Did you learn how to love?' I so want my answer to be yes."

Love comes before peace. That is a profound truth to consider.

Did you learn how to love? That is a profound question to grapple with.

All of us have uncertain futures. In times of difficulty we can get so focused on the valley around us that we miss what God wants to do in our life—and our children's lives—during that time.

When facing turmoil, people tend to choose one of two paths, don't they? Some are filled with frustration and anger over their trials, while others find supernatural peace amidst the storms. Some grow hard and cold; others find a love that they would never have understood apart from a time of pain.

Today, as Jeff and I and our children watch Aaron, it brings tears to our eyes. But not for the reason you would think. Yes, we have cried many times over the future that has been denied our friends. We have been angry with God for allowing them such a hard path. But mostly, when the tears come, it is because we see the precious love of Jesus shining through them. A love that leads Lara to serve her husband with sweetness and an eternal perspective every day. A love that leads Aaron to pray for our family and dozens of others throughout the day. A love that leads him to tell us, "I may not be able to do much more than pray for people and listen to and encourage Lara each day, but I'm going to try to be the best pray-er and encourager I can be."

What a key challenge for us and our children: Instead of making peace our ultimate goal, we should ask, *Am I learning how to love?* As we do, peace will come.

Prayer

God, You are love. Help our family learn how to develop and show Your love even when—especially when—things are difficult. I know that as we do that, we are revealing You to each other and to the world. Yet this choice to love requires sacrifice that I can't accomplish without Your Spirit. Spirit of God, I humbly submit to You. Fill me with Your love until I'm overflowing. This brings joy to my heart. And knowing that You are in my heart brings me peace. Amen.

What does it look like for you and your family to "learn how to love" in the midst of turmoil? When unwanted circumstances arise, what two or three things can you or your kids do differently? How can all of you keep those "learning how to love" actions in mind when things get hard?

NOTES

Day 10

One day the Pharisees asked Jesus, "When will the Kingdom of God come?" Jesus replied . . . "You won't be able to say, 'Here it is!' or 'It's over there!' For the Kingdom of God is already among you."
Luke 17:20–21, NLT

Part of the Kingdom

A few years ago, my goddaughter Nadine, an Air Force medic, was deployed to the Middle East. She had grown up constantly popping in and out of our home, giving her "young person" perspective as I wrote each of my books and, as she got older, staying with our young kids many weekends when Jeff and I were speaking out of town. Even though she was a strong, resilient woman, watching her go was hard.

Many people were praying for her. And she needed it, because she started off pretty miserable. The temperature was 116 degrees, and it hadn't rained for a year. Dust and sweat hung in the air. Sleep was constantly interrupted by calls to action. Inside massive C-130 cargo planes that took off and landed almost vertically to avoid surface-to-air missiles, Nadine was rattled by the regular flashes and bangs of decoy flares. Her crew would swoop in to some undisclosed area, pick up injured soldiers, and patch them up in flight for transfer to hospitals. She prayed that the soldiers—and everyone aboard—would make it home safely.

The flight crew finally had a break, but it was distressing in a different way. In a nearby city dripping with oil money and flashy shops, she saw constant poor treatment of others. She watched a man arrogantly walk along a luxury mall, followed by a string of burka-clad women with their heads down. In the parking garage, a male attendant refused to speak to or take money from a female driver trying to exit. Nadine was stuck there for hours until a man arrived to pay.

When Nadine returned to base, homesickness settled in like an unwelcome, unaccustomed fog. She missed her home, her church, her friends, and the security of being part of a community of faith. She felt so isolated and alone.

Nadine decided to seek out the base chaplain for counsel, and he beckoned her into his office. Just as she was about to pour out her heart, some brightly colored books caught her eye. Stunned, she saw our books—*For Women Only, For Men Only,* and others—there on the shelf. Books she had grown up helping with half a world away.

In that moment, she heard the still, small voice of God.

"Nadine, you're not isolated; You're part of the Kingdom of God. My Kingdom isn't in Atlanta. It is everywhere I am."

Just as suddenly as it had landed, the ugly homesickness lifted. She wasn't isolated at all!

As Nadine walked into the base's worship service soon thereafter, she saw military personnel of every color and background standing, hands lifted, singing the songs from back home. Worshiping the same God. Part of the same Kingdom. Brothers and sisters, no matter where they were.

Have you ever found yourself in unfamiliar territory? Maybe it's a literal move or maybe it's just a new job, new friends, or new season in relationships. Maybe you feel so alone during the day when the baby is sleeping and wonder what you're supposed to do with your life. Or maybe you feel like one of our readers, who said she was always busy with the kids but lonely within her marriage and desperately wanted to reconnect with her man again.

If you feel like you're in your very own desert and longing to feel seen and heard, take heart. You are not isolated! The Kingdom of God and His people are right where you are. Seek out those who can help and encourage you. But most of all, lay your weary burdens at His feet and watch how He provides refreshment right when you need it.

Prayer

Jesus, thank You for bringing the Kingdom of God to the world . . . and to me! Thank You for reminding me of the time you came to me through a friend. You helped her see my sadness and need and led her to reach out. Lord, whenever I am in need of support, please bring Your people my way. Help me to see how to reach out to others in need as well. But Lord, most of all help me to reach out for You. I am so grateful that You see me right where I am. Amen.

Was there a time recently when you felt isolated, lonely, or longing to feel seen and heard? Has there been a time when you know that God has reached out to you through a friend? In the future, how might you reach out for the connection you need?

NOTES

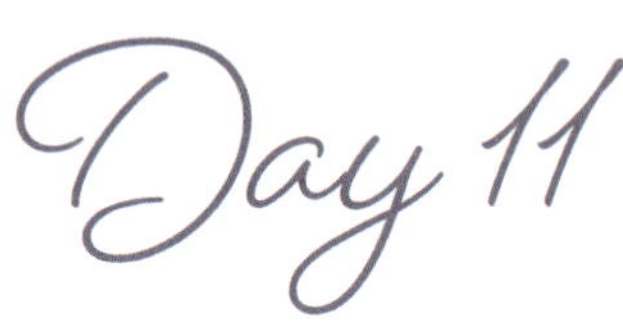

Do not be anxious about anything, but in everything by prayer and supplication with thanksgiving let your requests be made known to God. And the peace of God, which surpasses all understanding, will guard your hearts and your minds in Christ Jesus.
Philippians 4:6–7, ESV

Letting Go and Flying High

I'll never forget the day I heard my eighteen-month-old daughter shrieking. I sprinted out the door toward the playground beside our house. There was Jeff and there was our daughter, shrieking with delight as her daddy energetically pushed her swing so high that she was horizontal with the ground . . . and not in a safety seat!

My heart was jumping out of my chest as I raced forward. Our little girl was going to fly off and break her head or arm or rib or all of the above! How could Jeff be so reckless?!

I was ready to scoop her up and let my husband have it, when it suddenly felt as if God grabbed me by the scruff of my neck to stop me in my tracks.

Stop, I sensed.

But she's going to get hurt! Everything in me wanted to grab her.

Stop. Right now. She is with her father. He loves her. He will take care of her.

I had to physically turn around, shaking from the effort to stop myself. But I was also absolutely sure that God was telling me to back off.

In every culture worldwide, anthropologists have found that a father will let a toddler get three times further away than a mother will. Although there are exceptions, a man is generally built to see his child run, soar, and, at times quite literally, fly high. If his children stumble and scrape a knee, he says, "Get up! Keep going!" Women, on the other hand, are more likely to usher their little ones around. To nurture and protect. "Don't go there! You might fall!"

Neither wiring is wrong. The problem comes when we say our way is "right." When we get agitated because in our minds our child isn't being nurtured the right way. When we worry that our man isn't protecting them in the same way we would.

Ladies, we have to let go. We have to recognize that men *will do it differently*—and they are designed by God to do so! If we tell our man that he needs to do it our way, we're telling him that he's doing it wrong. And if we keep telling him that he is doing it wrong, he is going to back off. He will stop being engaged. Not only will our children miss something precious, but we will actually be *more* stressed! We may even start berating him for checking out as a father when, if we're honest, we wouldn't let him be a father.

Most fathers adore their children, just like we moms do. They don't want them hurt. They aren't foolhardy. They have much to give.

But they don't always feel adequate to the task. Men doubt themselves far more than we realize. Yet the answer isn't for us to tell them what to do. The answer is to encourage what they do, give them the freedom to make mistakes (just like we do!), and appreciate the great love and adventure they have to offer.

About fifteen minutes after I forced myself to go inside the house that day, Jeff came in, carrying our daughter upside down, still squealing. They were breathless and happy. If I had grabbed her away from him, it might have been the last time he took her to the playground.

Instead, I saw a dad who was pleased with himself and who loved being a dad.

Ladies, let's let go of the agitation that comes from always trying to control and instead recognize that our children are with a father—and a Heavenly Father—who loves them just as much as we do.

Prayer

Lord, You have made us different on purpose. Forgive me for not honoring those differences and instead trying to control how my man does things with our children. Give me the courage to set aside my opinions and trust him . . . and You. Show me the beauty of a father loving his children in the way he is designed to, and help me to show my man how much I really do appreciate him. Amen.

Reflect

Consider: Do you let the man in your life parent differently from you? Or is there an underlying feeling—or overt saying—that he's not doing it "right"? Spend the next two weeks purposefully letting him do things his way and simply appreciating what he does. Then, journal what happens.

NOTES

[Jesus' disciple said] "Here is a boy with five small barley loaves and two small fish, but how far will they go among so many?" . . . Jesus then took the loaves, gave thanks, and distributed to those who were seated as much as they wanted. . . . [They] filled twelve baskets with [what was] left over.

John 6:9–13

Bring What You Have

I was completely overwhelmed. I had never had so many different demands from so many different directions at once. A massive stroke had disabled my father; and my husband, my brother, and I had set many work deadlines aside to help my mom, who lived out of state. I was helping my parents as they prepared to move to our city and working with contractors to eventually build out our house for them.

At the same time, our ministry was going through a big staff transition. And by now, Jeff and I were seriously behind on our next research project and book deadlines.

We were also in an intense season with our children. Our son was starting high school, and we were sending our first child off to college. Much still had to be done in the week before moving Morgen into her dorm.

So many important needs . . . but one thing kept staring me in the face: The few squares on the calendar until the one marked "COLLEGE MOVE-IN DAY."

Morgen and I had planned several mom-daughter days. Not just for last minute preparations, but to lounge on the couch and watch silly romance movies. To get our nails done and eat at her favorite little cafes.

I was constantly fighting emotion; excited for her to spread her wings, but oh, how I would miss her. It was a joyful sort of grief.

Yet that grief was mixed with guilt and stress about being so behind on work. How could I ignore another work week? But how could I *not* spend these precious hours with her? I sent an email to friends, asking for prayer, but I had no peace.

Very soon, God used a friend to speak directly to my troubled heart. Her email said:

> You have been through SO MUCH with your dad's health AND remodeling AND the process of moving for them, on top of college and your work situation. I am PRAYING for you to rest on the river of His Holy Spirit and rely on Him to take you to what needs doing on each day. HE HAS THIS! He just needs your "five loaves and two fish" to make each day His miracle. You are not dropping balls! Or ignoring them! You are parenting eternal souls, honoring your father and mother, and He will continue to empower your stewardship of these work projects. You just have to do the "next right thing."

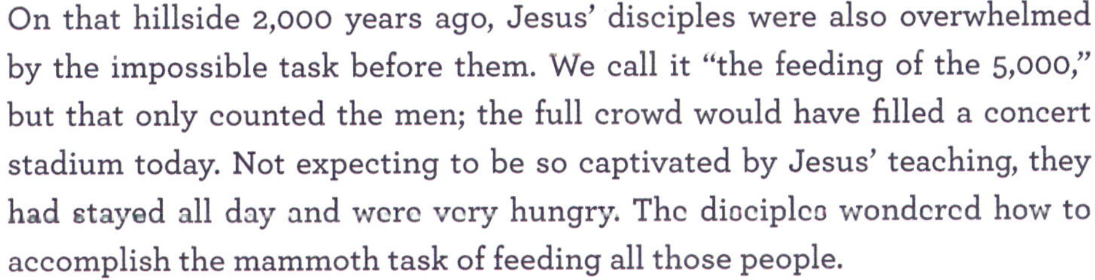

On that hillside 2,000 years ago, Jesus' disciples were also overwhelmed by the impossible task before them. We call it "the feeding of the 5,000," but that only counted the men; the full crowd would have filled a concert stadium today. Not expecting to be so captivated by Jesus' teaching, they had stayed all day and were very hungry. The disciples wondered how to accomplish the mammoth task of feeding all those people.

But they didn't have to accomplish it, and neither did the boy with the loaves and fish. All they had to do was bring what they had. To be faithful to do the next right thing they were being asked to do and let Jesus do what only He could do.

Sisters, when you are overwhelmed, don't try to accomplish it all. Just bring what you have and trust Jesus with the rest.

After breaking down in tears of thanks from reading my friend's email, I knew what my next right thing was: to shut off my computer, tell my parents that I'd be a little hard to reach the next few days, and go sit with my daughter to watch a movie. We had some precious, irreplaceable times together before the day Jeff and I waved goodbye and drove home into a new chapter of our lives. Yes, there were tears. But there was also peace.

Prayer

Jesus, the hours in my day don't seem like enough to take care of my obligations. My energy doesn't seem like enough. My skills don't seem enough. Lord, forgive me for thinking "my" part needs to be enough. You used five loaves and two fish to feed thousands, and You made a point to have much left over. I give what seem like my meager abilities to You. Lead me to the next right thing. I surrender this to You, trusting that You will do what only You can do! Amen.

Reflect

Is there a situation you feel completely ill-equipped to handle? How might this reminder to simply bring what you have and turn it over to God offer hope to your situation? What is the "next right thing" you can do today?

NOTES

Day 13

When anxiety was great within me,
your consolation brought me joy.
Psalm 94:19

When Worry Crosses the Line

Caroline was enjoying some conversation in the teacher's lounge when the department head suddenly revealed that enrollment was significantly down, and with it, funds from the state to operate.

"I think we're okay," he said, "but if the county gets nervous, we could see some teaching positions shift or get cut. Apparently, none of us is 'safe' until next week, right after Labor Day."

These words played over and over again in Caroline's mind during that long week. As a single mom, she was the only provider for her three kids. If her income went away, they literally could be out on the street within a month.

On the Saturday of Labor Day weekend, she opened her email to see this from her principal: "Can we talk Tuesday?"

Those four words were like a brick through the window of Caroline's heart. *Can we talk?* What could that possibly mean, other than it was time to be cut, or "shifted" out of her position?

The next day was a Labor Day picnic, but Caroline was in no mood to enjoy it. She hadn't slept a wink. She stayed moody and distracted, hardly enjoying the beautiful weather or her loved ones.

Tuesday arrived, and Caroline dragged herself to school. She went straight to the principal's office. "Good morning. You wanted to speak with me?"

Her principal looked up. "About what, again?"

"Your email said, 'Can we talk?'"

"Oh, right. Here, see this change the committee made on our website? Could you suggest a better word choice?"

Walking back to her classroom, Caroline didn't know whether to laugh or cry. All that worry! Had she really ruined a whole weekend based on a little bit of nothing?

"Lord," she whispered. "I can't handle that kind of emotional roller coaster! Can't You keep my heart from freaking out like this?"

And into her heart came these words. *Your choice, My child.*

She was suddenly washed with conviction. God tells us over and over that He is our provider. That He cares. That He is able. That we must make the choice not to worry about tomorrow. Yes, it is a human tendency to worry—but it is a human tendency that is based on a sinful habit of not trusting God.

Caroline's weekend of giving in to her whirling worries was really just a weekend of giving in to sin.

Women are particularly prone to this. In the survey of women for my book *For Men Only,* I discovered that 81 percent of us have trouble controlling those pop-up worries in our lives.

We can't always control the troubling concerns that come into our minds—whether it's about our job, our kids' grades, or the disagreement we had with our husband earlier in the day. But we *can* choose what we do with those thoughts once they appear.

Some people say, "That's just the way I am! I'm a worrier!" But think about how men and boys, who are hardwired to be visual, can be so tempted to look at all the inappropriate things that pop up in their field of vision. It is a biological impulse, but we tell our sons that they need to take every thought captive instead. That the temptations will come, but the question is what they choose to *do* with them.

It works the same way for us, sisters. Worry is a temptation. But we need to choose to stop those roiling thoughts, to hand those worries over to Him, to focus on God's promises and have peace. Peace is not the absence of conflict; it's the ability to entrust that conflict to the One who knows our story from beginning to end and will walk with us every step of the way.

Prayer

Lord, I confess the sin of allowing worries to swirl in my head. You deserve better from me. You have always been there, and You have promised to provide for my every need. You have begged me to not worry about tomorrow, and yet I almost seem to want to indulge in those exact worries. Please forgive me, Lord. Wash my mind and heart clean and help me give the worries back to You every time they arise. I trust You, Lord. Amen.

Reflect

What is one worry that seems to always want to pop into your heart and mind these days? Take a moment to ask God to take the burden from you and declare your trust that He will see you through it. Commit that when you find it popping into your head going forward, you'll stop and give it back to the Lord.

NOTES

Day 14

A glad heart makes a cheerful face.
Proverbs 15:13, ESV

Face Training

Ariana looked around the walls of the sunroom. Her friend had hung frame after frame of family beach pictures. They spanned the years, starting with the kids as little, barely-walking toddlers to now taller-than-their-parents teenagers. But she was momentarily puzzled. She recognized the kids and the husband, but who was the woman with them? Embarrassed, she quickly realized it was her friend! Of course—who else would it be?

The issue was that her friend was *smiling* in the pictures. In everyday life, her friend rarely had a smile on her face, instead hosting a slightly dissatisfied expression. Which was why Ariana didn't immediately recognize this lovely, joyful, smiling woman as her. *I wonder if she realizes just how beautiful—inside and out—her smile makes her look,* Ariana thought with a tinge of judgment.

Suddenly, she remembered something that recently happened at her own job. She was walking down the hallway, deep in thought, when a male coworker stopped her.

"Can I ask you something?" he said. "Is there a reason you don't like me?" He went on to explain that Ariana gave him a weird look—almost a scowl—whenever they passed each other.

"What? You thought I didn't like you?" Ariana asked incredulously. "I like you a lot!"

"Oh, okay," her colleague said. "I guess you are just thinking serious thoughts, and I read it the wrong way. Never mind."

Now, standing in her friend's sunroom, Ariana realized she *was* pretty serious and focused at work. Being serious all the time was probably as off-putting to others as the dissatisfied expression her friend wore. Even more important, she thought with chagrin, having a default "serious" countenance was seen as being negative, which meant her life was certainly not reflecting the love of Christ or the joy of following Him.

And that might even be the case at home. She was already worried that her teenage son might feel like she was constantly judging him, when what he most needed was kindness and encouragement.

Ariana decided that her countenance needed to reflect on the outside the love and joy she had on the inside. But the next few days, she was surprised to discover that it didn't come easy. She literally had to train her face to lighten up. She began making it a practice to smile at people at work. And out in public. And at home with her family.

On the third day of making sure she smiled at her fifteen-year-old son, he looked at her and said, "What?"

"What do you mean?" Ariana asked.

"Why are you looking at me that way these days?" her son asked skeptically.

"Because I like you, and I'm proud of you," she answered.

"Huh," was the reply. But there was a little smile behind his eye rolling.

Ariana realized that sharing a genuine smile was a conscious, active choice she had to make. For a while, she felt silly. But she found that having a joyful expression actually made her feel more joyful. The more she did it, the better results she got.

And why wouldn't she? Jesus said, "You are the light of the world.... People [do not] light a lamp and put it under a basket, but on a stand, and it gives light to all in the house. In the same way, let your light shine before others, so that they may see your good works and give glory to your Father who is in heaven" (Matthew 5:14-16, ESV). The Spirit of God lives within us! We must never let His light be hidden by routinely stressed-out, serious, bored, or annoyed expressions. Let our expressions reflect the hope we have within.

Prayer

Oh, Lord, thank You for the joy You give me and the love that is in my life because of You. Forgive me for so easily getting consumed with the details of the day that I focus on everything but You. Lord, help me feel Your joy and love every day. And let my expression and words reflect it. Make me a light to this world that so deeply needs it—especially to my own family. Amen.

Reflect

When others look at you, do they mostly see the joy and love within you? Or is it more likely that they see an expression that reflects concentration, seriousness, focus, dissatisfaction, boredom, or something else? If you need to purposefully smile more often, write down three different ways you can remember to do that—and then put them into practice.

NOTES

Day 15

Unless the Lord *builds the house, the builders labor in vain. Unless the* Lord *watches over the city, the guards stand watch in vain.*

Psalm 127:1

Angels Standing Guard

Long before I wrote my current relationship research books, I wrote several novels, including one called *The Veritas Conflict*. These were spiritual thrillers imagining the spiritual battles around believers. I wanted my descriptions of angels and demons to be very biblical so they were as accurate as possible. But how to do that, given that spiritual warfare is not explicitly described in depth in the Bible?

I sent out an email to a small group of godly, mature, and very trustworthy friends asking for private connections to other godly, mature, and very trustworthy individuals. I was looking for people who had actually seen angels or witnessed their presence in some way. I heard back from eight people who had credible stories to share. These firsthand accounts were eye opening and a tremendous resource for the novel. Tamara's story was particularly memorable.

Tamara shared how her sixteen-year-old daughter, Elizabeth, had spent a year being stalked by an ex-boyfriend. He had become abusive and unstable, and when Elizabeth tried to break up with him, he became more so. Soon he lashed out with regular threats of specific violent, sexual action against her. The family got a restraining order, but the threats continued. Their daughter privately moved schools. She changed jobs, only to see him across the road when she left at night. She got whispered threats over the phone. Then a note appeared on her locker. He had found her new school.

The family was living in absolute fear.

One day Tamara got on her knees and cried out to God in a loud voice, "Lord, I can't live like this! We've done everything we can think of to protect our family! You promise to be with us, but how do I know You're really protecting us now?"

At that moment, Tamara heard that still, small voice in her spirit: *Look out your window.*

Shakily, Tamara went to the window, slowly pulled the curtain back, and nearly shrieked in a moment of heart-stopping awe and fear.

Standing guard over their home—right in the middle of their cul-de-sac—was a twenty- or thirty-foot-tall angel, shining with the glory of the Lord. He was terrifying and glorious and stared right at her.

He was visible for only a few moments. As she backed away from the window, shaking from head to foot, Tamara understood why most angelic visitations in the Bible began with the words, "Fear not!" The awesome reality of the heavenly host and the Psalm 91:11 promise that "He will command his angels . . . to guard you in all your ways," was suddenly powerful, and majestic, and comforting beyond all comprehension.

Nothing was getting to them without going through God's hand first.

In 2 Kings 6, the prophet Elisha's servant is paralyzed with fear as he sees the enemy surrounding his city. Unfazed, Elisha assures him that there is an even greater army protecting them. God opens the servant's eyes, and he sees that the hills are full of "horses and chariots of fire."

Perhaps you're facing some spiritual warfare right now. Maybe, like Tamara, you're crying out to God for a child who seems to be nearly in the enemy's clutches. No matter what the battle, be assured, like Elisha's servant, that "those who are for us are far greater than those arrayed against us."

There is an angel army, and Christ Himself is captain of the host. While it's certainly wise to do our best to protect our families, our human efforts are merely that—human. We can take comfort in the fact that Christ is our victorious Savior, the leader of angel armies, the One whose promises and protections never fail!

Prayer

Lord, I am so grateful that You are the God of heaven's armies. That You love us so much, Your mighty warriors fight on our behalf against the spiritual forces of darkness. Father, when times of fear come, remind me that unless You protect our family, all our watching and worrying is in vain. But remind me that You do protect our family. Help me learn to trust in You. Amen.

In what way has your heart been fearful lately? If you could see into the spiritual realm and see the reality of God's promises to have angels "guard all your ways," how would that impact your fear? Write down those thoughts and reassurances, and come back to this page the next time you are fearful.

NOTES

Day 16

And David was greatly distressed . . . but [he] encouraged himself in the Lord his God.
1 Samuel 30:6, KJV

Encourage Yourself in the Lord Instead

I was stepping offstage after speaking at a women's conference when the phone rang. My dad was having a stroke and being rushed to the hospital.

As the church's leaders scrambled to get me to the airport, my thoughts were racing. I was in the middle of an extraordinarily busy travel season, launching two major book projects, and battling bronchitis. I was spent, empty, and exhausted, and now the news of my precious father's stroke. *This can't be happening,* I thought. My parents had just been finalizing plans to move from Virginia to a beautiful independent living community near our family where they could enjoy the next season of their lives.

Was that all now gone?

On the plane, I searched medical sites, trying to get a handle on his odds. Symptoms, causes, and complications swirled by in a tornado of bad news. Then, for the first hours at the hospital, whenever my father was sleeping, I would talk to doctors and nurses, researching possibilities.

My anxious thoughts multiplied. Though research was my thing (after all, hadn't I written a dozen research-based books?), my frantic findings were certainly not calming my soul.

Perhaps you know the feeling. Even without a jolting emergency call, we've all had news that risks sending us into a tailspin. Your son tells you his SAT score, and your heart stops. You pull out your phone or computer to search options, as you suddenly realize he might not get into that good state school you've been planning on. How will you afford private colleges? How likely is tutoring to pull his score up?

Or maybe a spiteful classmate accuses your middle-school daughter of cheating, and she's at risk of being expelled. There must be some way you can defend her! Can you find a good witness to her innocence?

Those "I've got to figure it out" feelings can spring us into action and get our fix-it fingers flying across the keyboard. But although we do all that figuring and fixing in order to feel better, we rarely do.

Why?

After those first few frantic days with my father, I began to be convicted. Yes, I had been praying, but my actions showed where my trust was really placed. I had been relying more on Google than on God. More on the wisdom of doctors than in the Great Physician.

The Bible contrasts how King Saul and David handled worrisome news. When Saul heard the Philistine army was approaching, he was so tense and worried—so deeply wanted to know what was going to happen and how to "figure it out"—that he consulted a medium. David confronted a much worse piece of news: His enemies had burned their towns and carried off their women, including David's wives. David's bitter men wanted to stone him! David was hurting, but he didn't try to figure and fix. Instead, the Bible says that David "encouraged himself in the Lord."

Perhaps he sang a worship song he had composed. Maybe he whispered a psalm written while tending sheep. Maybe he ran his mind over the many examples of God's faithfulness in the past. As he did, not only did the Lord bring peace, He gave battle strategy and eventual victory.

Most of us won't look for actual fortune-tellers when we're worried, but aren't we doing a version of it when we scramble to figure out chances, and possibilities, and fixes for our problems? I confess I've probably turned to Google before God in many a crisis.

I don't know how my father's health and future will play out. But I've seen the Lord be faithful over and over again. Peace will always replace anxiety when we remember that. When we set aside our need to figure it all out and encourage ourselves in the Lord instead.

Prayer

Lord, forgive me. Too often I immediately turn to other things for help when I'm feeling distressed, as if the results are up to me. Lord, spur me to run to You with my troubled heart. I know that is where I will find encouragement, comfort, and peace. I know I can trust You to guide me as I watch events unfold under Your sovereign care. Amen.

Reflect

In times of trouble, have you ever felt that you just need to find the right answer and you'll feel better? Next time you find yourself scouring the Internet for clues or asking friends or counselors, how can you remind yourself to pause and ask God for help first—and on an ongoing basis? What difference will it make if you do?

NOTES

Day 17

"For I know the plans I have for you," declares the Lord, "plans to prosper you and not to harm you, plans to give you hope and a future."
Jeremiah 29:11

There's a Plan for Every Child

Abby dreaded mornings at the bus stop. Living in an affluent area with excellent schools, most kids were highly academic. They were on the fast track for college and worldly success. Conversation among the moms often revolved around their gifted children, AP classes, extra-curricular activities, and their children's latest successes.

"Did you hear that little Joel got asked to join the middle school robotics team already?"

"We were so proud of Zoe for getting a space in that Ivy League summer program."

"Did I mention Nate was placed into the group reading at a third-grade level?"

Abby listened, and nodded, and congratulated . . . and quailed inside. She and her husband had adopted their eight-year-old son from a run-down orphanage when he was three years old. A few weeks into his third-grade year, she still wasn't sure if he would ever be able to read. He certainly wasn't on the fast track for college. Although God could do miracles, it was unlikely her son would experience the same academic achievements as these other kids.

Standing at the bus stop day after day, listening to those exchanges, she got more and more discouraged. It was hard not to compare. Every excited anecdote from another mom seemed to subtly imply that her own son was somehow "less than."

It hurt.

It is so easy to subconsciously compare whether our children "measure up" to the world's standards of success, achievement, or accomplishment. We can end up feeling "less than" ourselves because we feel somehow responsible for the challenges they face.

Which is really silly if you think about it. God gave us our child, and He has a specific plan and purpose for them—just like He does for every other child at the bus stop. It may not look the same, but if it is *His* plan, there is not one smidge of "less" about it.

Eventually, God opened Abby's eyes to the main cause of her stress. She was taking a huge amount of her son's struggle personally, thinking it was her responsibility to fix it. And when she couldn't, she was frustrated, sad, even depressed. The bus stop chatter was a constant reminder of "her" failures.

That all changed when she saw the passage from Jeremiah in a new light. God created her son, and He knew he would spend time in an orphanage without the ideal amount of stimulation for brain development. God knew this boy would be adopted by Abby and her husband. He had *plans* for her son! God wasn't freaking out that her son couldn't yet read. He knew exactly how He was going to accomplish His purposes in and through his life.

Abby's son didn't need to have a certain level of academic ability to be valuable. God bestows many types of gifts. My friend realized that every year her son's teachers mentioned the same qualities about him: He is sweet, kind, and caring. If he sees another student hurting, he reaches out to help. He is such a hard worker.

By the end of the year, there were tears in Abby's eyes as her son's teachers nominated him for a state-level "exceptional children" award for his willingness to always give 110 percent.

In God's eyes, her son's value was as great as those who might see greater worldly success. According to *God's* standards, every human being is of priceless value. To paraphrase Psalm 139, our children are wonderfully made, and God's works are wonderful. All of their days—and His plans—are written in God's book before a single one of them comes to be.

Prayer

Lord, You are the good Father who created my children. You know their strengths and weaknesses intimately, and You knew they would be mine. Lord, help me remember that every experience, challenge, and success they have was mapped by You long before they were ever born. I release all of my worries to You, O Lord: Your plans are best, and in that, I will rest. Amen.

Reflect

Does your child struggle in some way with achievement, competency, or success? Do you wonder what your child's place and purpose in this world will be? Consider what you focus on in estimating your child's potential in life. Do you judge by the world's standards of status and achievement or God's standards? Appreciate your child's priceless value and know that God created them uniquely for the plan He has for their life.

NOTES

Day 18

See, I am doing a new thing! Now it springs up; do you not perceive it?
Isaiah 43:19

The Best Is Yet to Come

I still remember the conference volunteer who picked me up at the airport when my kids were small. When she said she had four teenagers, I replied, as many people would, "Oh my! Bless you! How are you surviving?"

I had the impression that the "adolescent years" were something to brace for. I dreaded the idea of my sweet little ones morphing into distant and disrespectful teens.

The volunteer smiled. "I have to tell you: I think that stereotype is so wrong. And dangerous. I absolutely loved when my kids were small, and I love the teenage stage even more. Sure, there are challenges, but there are challenges in *every* stage. Every season with my kids has been better than the one before."

She shared her belief that God wants us to expect a beautiful progression in every stage, and that if you expect difficulties instead (terrible twos, threen-agers, difficult tweens, disrespectful and moody teens, etc.), those are what you'll notice—and probably overreact to!

Her philosophy was to look forward to every season of parenting and enjoy the blessings of each one.

I can honestly say that no other single piece of advice has affected my view of parenting more.

A number of years later, my ten-year-old daughter and I were driving in our minivan when she gave me her first real eye roll in response to something I said. Now, normally, my head explodes at signs of disrespect—and so does my voice! But suddenly, it was as if God flashed my mind back to my conversation with that mom.

I took a moment to be calm, and said, "Honey, let's have a conversation about this. You may not realize it, but you were really disrespectful right there, and that's not okay. I know you think dad and I just have random rules, and we don't understand you. You think that we don't know what we're talking about. And you might have those feelings again. So here's my request: Can you have grace with us for, oh, about the next ten years?"

My daughter laughed, but then stopped as she realized I meant it. "I'm serious, honey. Can we agree that until you go off to college, whenever you think we don't know what we're talking about, you'll have grace with us? Because otherwise, these next ten years might be unpleasant for all of us."

She looked at me for a minute. I could tell she was suddenly taking my request seriously.

"Okay," she said. No eye roll in sight.

When another eye roll made an appearance, I reminded her, "Remember our discussion? That isn't okay. And this is one of those times when you can show grace."

When Jeff and I started looking at parenting this way, we had peace instead of stress and anger. Although we wouldn't let poor behavior slide, we were determined to address it with calmness, humor, and logic instead of highly charged emotion. And because we didn't jump all over her, our daughter was more willing to listen to what we had to say.

We still had high expectations for our kids, but they were reasonable expectations. We had begun to anticipate the best—not the worst—through the various stages of their lives.

As we journey through the seasons of our children's lives, rather than dreading the coming stage or clinging to the current one (how many times have we posted, "Stop growing up!" on social media?), let's be excited about how our kids are changing and who they're becoming. Transforming our outlook will transform our interactions with them. Yes, they might have difficult moments, but let's anticipate that we will not only get through those seasons, we'll also *enjoy* them.

Relax, moms, and take heart—the best is yet to come!

Prayer

Lord, help me not be impacted by the negative expectations that I hear. Instead, help me to be transformed by the renewing of my mind. Give me Your thoughts and perceptions of the season I am in and the ones to come. Help me to anticipate Your goodness through all of it and receive the blessing and peace You have for me instead of the stress I so often bring upon myself. Jesus, help me to meditate on Your ways and not the world's ways for my kids. I thank You that this is Your heart for me—and for them. Amen.

Do you find yourself dreading certain stages in the life of your kids because of what you've heard or read about those ages? Instead, consider this question: What would it look like to expect the best of the next stage? What can you do to prepare to have that outlook?

NOTES

I have told you these things, so that in me you may have peace. In this world you will have trouble. But take heart! I have overcome the world.
John 16:33

Created to Worship

"Whoa! What's going on?" the Uber driver asked Anna.

"What do you mean?" she answered.

"When you got in my car, something came in with you!" he answered.

Clearly at a loss, he adjusted his baseball cap as he peered at his passenger in the rearview mirror. "I don't even know how to describe it," the driver stammered. "Is it the Holy Spirit or something?"

He seemed confounded that he had even uttered those words.

Anna smiled. "That's exactly Who it is," she answered, herself confounded at the words that were tumbling out of her mouth. "I've just spent three days in a worship conference, worshiping the one true God. I guess you're getting a little taste of the heaven I just experienced."

An uncharacteristic boldness poured out of her.

"As a matter of fact," she continued, leaning forward, "I'm guessing it's no mistake God put me into your car. Do you have any idea how much He loves you?"

At this, her driver burst into tears.

"I was told that a long time ago," he said. "But I didn't believe it."

It took only minutes for him to hear the good news of God's love—and to pray for salvation right then and there. Anna couldn't believe it! This had never happened to her before! She was on a Holy Spirit high.

After saying goodbye at the airport, she headed through security to fly home . . . and felt the swelling balloon inside her begin to leak.

For three days she had been at a worship conference with amazing worship bands and speakers. And now she was about to resume "real life"—a life that had included some serious storms. Two months before, a tornado had ripped through their neighborhood and damaged their home. Shortly thereafter, Anna's husband, Ted, was betrayed by a business partner and fleeced out of their savings. And soon after that, Ted's father died.

Ted had insisted she stick with her long-planned trip to meet friends at this worship conference. But now she was going home to a grieving husband and children who were surely watching to see how Christians respond to crises.

Anna and Ted were determined that the kids see their parents on their knees. They wanted their children to witness not a stale religion, but a fiery faith. And yet all that fire in Anna started to flicker and burn low as she went through airport security, her mind turning away from her days of worship and toward "real life."

Which is when she realized: It didn't have to be that way. She didn't have to attend a worship conference to worship the one true God! She didn't have to listen to great speakers share their insight in order to praise the God whose understanding is infinite. After all, what greater gift could she and Ted give their children than to see parents who not only *prayed* in the midst of the storm but *worshiped* the God of the storm?!

That night back at home, Priscilla, Anna's middle school daughter, mentioned the youth pastor's sermon. "He said God created the universe in such precise ways! Did you know there's a very precise amount of salt in the ocean? If it were 1 percent lower or higher, all the fish would die! And if the earth was a tiny bit closer to the sun, all life would be burned up. A little further away and the earth would be frozen! Isn't God amazing?"

Yes, Priscilla, God is amazing, Anna thought.

Sisters, we can trust this One who cares for us with such precision. And worshiping Him, saying, "You are amazing, God," will take our mind off our worries and put it firmly where it belongs.

Prayer

Lord, our understanding is imperfect, but You are perfect! You created us and care for us with such beautiful precision. Bring to my mind, every day, throughout the day, all the amazing things You do for me and my family. Cause us to worship You for who You are and what You have done. May our family and everyone we come into contact with be changed as we behold Your glory! Amen.

Reflect

How can you remember to worship and praise God when worries come to mind? Write down three different ideas. Then implement them this week and journal what happens.

NOTES

Day 20

From the ends of the earth I call to you, I call as my heart grows faint; lead me to the rock that is higher than I.
Psalm 61:2

The Heart of the Matter

Polly and Sam spent the morning chasing three small children around and gleefully talking about the arrival of their fourth. They spent the evening in shock.

"Your baby has a very rare heart defect—maybe more than one." The doctor broke the news as gently as he could.

It was a stunning blow. Gone were the plans of giving birth to a healthy, full-term baby. They were now looking at weeks in the NICU—if their son even survived the first few hours. If he did, once he reached the whopping size of 4 pounds, 7 ounces, he would have major open-heart surgery—on a heart the size of a Cheerio. If he survived that, he would need an even more intense open-heart surgery to fix the final defects.

Lord! Lord! Polly could hardly even pray, other than the most primal cries in God's direction. Her thoughts and feelings were numb. There was literally nothing she could do to affect the outcome.

Every day, Polly and Sam prayed that God would keep that baby safe for one more precious day of *in utero* development. They prayed for healing. They tried to have a semblance of normalcy for their other kids. And every day, they had to decide whether they were going to lean on God in the most foundational way possible: to cling to Him, believe in His goodness, and trust Him no matter the outcome.

At thirty-two weeks, little William was born. He was diagnosed with not one but three rare heart defects. His life hung in the balance. *Lord! Lord!*

The first few days, when fear threatened to swamp them, over and over again, Polly and Sam simply tried to cling to the Rock. And over and over again they felt the love of the Father in the midst of procedures and turmoil, sleepless nights and stressful days. It was as if God was making a point of giving them His peace.

A few days later, the surgeon brought in a picture and pointed to a specific part of the heart. This, he explained, is the defect that saved William's life. Polly and Sam looked at him quizzically.

The doctor explained that the first two defects were dead ends in the heart. There was no possibility for blood to flow. The baby would not have survived in utero. But the third defect was a hole. A miraculous hole that allowed blood to flow through the heart to the rest of the body. A hole that allowed William to grow in utero. That gave him the chance to be born. To have surgery. To fix the dead ends.

As they stroked their baby's tiny arms and legs that night, they gave thanks to God. The defects were there. But so was their little boy.

During their weeks in the hospital, Polly and Sam proclaimed God's goodness. They not only clung to their Rock, they wanted to introduce Him to everyone else! From friends to doctors to nurses to hospital staff, they told everyone the story.

They could have chosen to focus on the three heart defects and the long, challenging, risky road ahead. Instead, they focused on that one miracle defect that allowed William to be born in the first place. That showed that God was working. They didn't understand why He allowed the challenges, but they knew He brought this child here for a specific purpose.

When we find ourselves facing fear over our kids' health and future, we have a choice. Instead of reacting out of panic and anger, we can cling to the Rock that is higher than the waves threatening to wash us out to a dark sea. And as we do, we will see what our great God is doing and the peace He brings, even in the storm.

Prayer

Lord, there are days when storms swirl around me. When my heart grows faint and fear threatens to swamp me. But You are the Rock that is higher than I. Lord, in those moments I ask that You would lead me to Yourself. And in those moments, help me to truly see what You are doing. Help me to see the ways You are working. Show me, Lord, that even in the storm, You are always, always at work out of your great love for me. I love you, Lord. I am so grateful that my heart grows faint but Yours never does. Amen.

Is there anything you are fearful or worried about now in regard to your child that might be distracting you from seeing God at work? Stop right now and write down those fears and how you might cling to the Rock in the storm. In the days to come, as God reveals what He is doing, make it a point to come back to this page and write those down.

NOTES

Do not despise these small beginnings,
for the Lord rejoices to see the work begin.
Zechariah 4:10, NLT

Don't Despise the Small Beginnings

My friend Elena was watching the chapel at her kids' Christian school when God's voice broke through. Now that her kids were older, she knew she had more to give. She had asked the Lord to make clear where she could serve.

I should explain that Elena is an *extremely* competent woman. She is one of those people that can somehow keep fourteen different plates spinning smoothly, all with a cheerful smile on her face. Although she would never say it out loud, she knew she was skilled at organization and leadership. She didn't want a full-time job just yet but felt that God had something special for her. She just needed to be patient, and His plans would be made clear.

She pondered teaching, organizing, or leading something new at their influential school. *Somewhere I could bless the school community,* she thought.

And in an instant at that student chapel, she suddenly knew.

Pray for Jodie.

"Okay, Lord," she said to God, "Got it. What else?"

Pray for Jodie.

"Wait—that's it? Don't you want me to work at the school? What *job* do you want me to have?"

Pray for Jodie.

Elena realized that God *was* giving her a job: to pray for just one person. Jodie was an acquaintance with four active kids who worked part-time at the school and whose husband had a much-more-than-full-time job: He was the headmaster.

Pray faithfully for her, God whispered.

It took faith—and a little humility—for Elena to agree. But over the course of the next year, she learned that God wasn't using her in the "big" ways Elena had imagined, but in the little ways that mattered intensely to one person.

Elena was able to walk with Jodie through a very important year in her life and the life of the school. She praised God in Jodie's victories, was a prayer warrior during stressful times, and stood in the gap when Jodie didn't even know how to pray. And Jodie in turn stepped up to pray for Elena. They grew immensely close.

God used Elena to bring peace into another mom's life at a vulnerable time. And with it, peace to a headmaster and a whole school.

Have you ever prayed expectantly, only to receive an answer that you *didn't* expect? It can be hard to accept those! And yet God can take our small steps of faith and magnify them into blessings—not just for others, but for us.

As you can imagine, Elena's assignment quickly became a great treasure. He didn't just bring her a ministry; He gave her a strong friendship and prayer partnership that has lasted for years and has proven to be a continually life-affirming gift.

When we look at what's ahead in life, we tend to focus on the large moments—the major projects, mission trips, and career highlights. But when we listen for the still, small voice of God, He is far more likely to direct us to a journey of seemingly modest moments that have far-reaching eternal impacts. Like listening to a child who feels she doesn't have any friends and helping her be the one person in her class who welcomes everyone. Like driving kids to community activities and jobs day after day, places where they can be a light in a dark world. Like praying for a friend week in, week out, and watching God's hand move in an entire school because of it.

Our big God can take our small seeds and spread them out; He multiplies His great love. And usually, that love comes back to us as well.

Prayer

Lord, help me not despise the small beginnings. Is there anything You would have me do that I've been resisting or setting aside because it doesn't seem to matter? Something that would lead to a blessing for others or for me? Bring those things to mind right now, Lord. And forgive me for not prioritizing them, as You would have me do. I commit to You, Jesus, that I will step out in those ways as You show me how. Even though I can only see a glimpse of it, thank You for the blessing of being part of Your great plan. Amen.

Reflect

Is God calling you to take a step to be faithful in some small things? Is there anything that you haven't seen as a big deal that might be a very big deal in God's plan? Take a moment and ask Him to open your eyes to those things, and write down anything that God brings to mind.

NOTES

Day 22

Two are better than one, because they have a good return for their labor. For if either of them falls, the one will lift up [her] companion.
Ecclesiastes 4:9–10, NASB

Finding the Club

Even before Julia got pregnant, she knew she would breastfeed her kids. In fact, she later confessed that she had so strongly believed it was the only right and healthy way to feed a baby that she secretly felt it was *wrong* not to nurse. In her private view, women who had issues with nursing just didn't try hard enough.

All too soon, she was brought face-to-face with both her judgments and an emotionally difficult, lonely season that was hard for her friends and family to understand. Her first child simply wouldn't nurse. Severe medical problems—an unplanned C-section, severe jaundice, and postpartum preeclampsia—turned joy into stress and sadness. Between the bottle-feeding necessary for improving the jaundice and treatments for the postpartum preeclampsia, her baby refused all breastfeeding. Every nurse and lactation consultant tried their magic, but nothing worked. Julia had plenty of milk, but even though her son would take a bottle, he simply wouldn't nurse.

So Julia began to pump. Every three hours around the clock, she would pump, and then someone would give her baby a bottle. She knew in her head that her baby was getting the nutrition he needed, but her heart was crying out with desperate disappointment, worry, and sadness. Why couldn't she do this most basic of motherly functions? Was this going to affect her bonding with her son?

She noticed judgmental looks from other women when she bottle-fed him in public. She recognized that she had been guilty of the same thing, and that made the disappointment, isolation, and loneliness even worse. Especially because many of her friends simply didn't understand why she was upset.

You may have felt that same sense that no one understands what you're going through. Maybe you feel like the odd mom out on the playground when other women seem like they've known each other since high school. Maybe you feel like the only working mom who can't volunteer for the class field trip, or the only single mom in a room full of women chattering about their husbands. Perhaps no one understands what it takes to care for a child with special needs.

Julia realized she *had* to find someone who understood. One day she came across an online group for women in her exact situation. As she scrolled through their posts and pictures, Julia knew she had found her home. Every mother there was exclusively pumping. No one was posting pictures of babies nursing. They were kind, compassionate, and welcoming to questions. Friendships, messages of support, and a community grew where women were loved and encouraged.

Five years later, Julia is still friends with many of those women, celebrating joys and mourning sorrows. When she had her second baby right after her husband had lost his job, one of these friends sent her a beautiful quilt. Another mom sent her a brand-new Pack 'n Play.

Motherhood may present us with struggles or circumstances we did not anticipate or ask for. We may be asked to join a club we never intended to be a member of. But the key is: *The club is there.* God asks us to find and connect with those who can lift each other up.

C. S. Lewis once said, “Friendship is born at that moment when one person says to another: ‘What! You too? I thought I was the only one.’” What a gift it is to link arms and say, “you too?”

When we are vulnerable in our need and reach out to others, God brings the peace of friendship to hurting hearts. God took away something Julia didn’t know she could lose and gave her something far greater.

Prayer

Lord, the words in the verse, “that we may be mutually encouraged” (Romans 1:12, ESV) resonate with my soul. That’s what I long for, to connect with people in positive, life-giving ways that strengthen them and me. So many interactions—like surface chitchat after church or shallow social media comments—are far too convenient in offering me pseudo-connections that leave me empty. Help me to find true, real connections with the people You have for me. Amen.

Reflect

What is one area of your life where you feel that most people simply don't understand what you're going through? Do you have one or more friends who *do* get it? If so, recommit to connecting with them. If not, write down two or three things you will do to find and connect with several women who get it and will support each other.

NOTES

Day 23

A man's heart plans his way,
but the Lord directs his steps.
Proverbs 16:9, NKJV

What Our Hearts Are Set On

Cassie's future was within her grasp, and then it all fell apart. She had loved volleyball since fifth grade. Colleges were competing to offer full-ride scholarships. Until the day she came down wrong, and somehow, in one bizarre, unfathomable moment, her foot shattered. Not her ankle, her *foot*. Multiple surgeries later, her volleyball career was over.

I met this devastated young woman and her mother at a church reception. Choking back tears, her mother said, "We are trying to trust the Lord in this. But I don't know how to encourage her."

My eyes filled with tears as a memory came to mind. "This is not nearly as hard as what you are going through, but would you mind if I told you a story?"

Twenty years before, as a new follower of Christ, I had started grad school at Harvard and made it through three layers of auditions for the famed Harvard-Radcliffe Collegium, the university's demanding traveling choir. I had long planned to do just two things in grad school: study for my master's degree and be a part of this choir. I wouldn't have time for other friendships or be able to attend Christian fellowship meetings, but I had sung competitively my whole life; it was a huge part of my identity.

Moments before I was called into the final audition (which was mostly to make sure I gelled with existing choir members) I realized, *Huh, I haven't prayed about this*. I quickly prayed, "Lord, I'm sorry I didn't think to ask. If You want me in the Collegium, let this go well. If not, let Your will be done." As I walked in, I felt a warm glow as the other choir members said, "We've heard a lot about you. It'll be nice to have a grad student in the group!"

The warm glow didn't last long. I literally couldn't sing any of the right notes. The director laughed and said, "You must just be nervous. Start again from the 'A.'" But I couldn't sing an A . . . or anything else, really. Finally, mercifully, the director cut the audition short. Mortified, I escaped the room and dissolved into tears as my plans crumbled around me.

Two weeks later, I went to a Christian Fellowship meeting and then joined their a cappella group. One of the tenors was a cute law student named Jeff Feldhahn. I would never have met him if God had spared me that time of anguish and allowed my plan to become reality.

As I recounted the story to that devastated mom and daughter twenty years later, I could see their recognition that, as the daughter said, "I know His plans are always better. But it just hurts."

As moms, we hurt when our children do. It hurts to watch our normally confident boy walk in the door with his head hanging low after football tryouts. Or our enthusiastic daughter sobbing when the debate team emails the final roster, and her name isn't on it. In a way, we can be even more devastated than they are.

But what if we step back and review the times in life we've been disappointed? What lessons did we learn? How did God use that experience for His glory and His plan for our lives?

Kids love hearing vulnerable stories from their parents, and as we describe what God did in those moments, we remind both our kids and ourselves of God's faithfulness. Yes, when we don't get something our heart was set on, we want to crawl into a hole and stay there. But it is *our* plans that have been disappointed, not God's. He is directing our steps to beautiful places our hearts could never have imagined on our own.

Prayer

Father, there have been many times I really wanted a different outcome than the one I got. Yet You met me in my disappointment and gave me something I couldn't have foreseen. Amazing God, help me hold my plans loosely, remembering that Your path for me is always best. May I be able to encourage my loved ones in the same way. Amen.

Think back on a time when God's plan was different than your own. What are some blessings that you now see came from it? How can that help you face those times when your expectations—or your children's—aren't going according to plan?

NOTES

Day 24

Trust in the Lord with all your heart, and do not lean on your own understanding. In all your ways acknowledge him, and he will make straight your paths.
Proverbs 3:5–6, ESV

(Not) The Life I Imagined

"Your daughter has serious national potential."

The famous former Olympian presented her evaluation as they waited for Kelly's eight-year-old daughter to finish practice at the county gymnastics center. "But she will have to get into intense one-on-one coaching at that Olympic feeder gym right away. She's gone as far as she can go here."

Kelly's heart was in turmoil as she drove away, Marissa happily chattering in the back seat. There was no way they could afford an Olympic-caliber private coach. She and her husband worked multiple jobs, and sporadic periods of unemployment in his construction work had taken a toll.

The comfortable life she had imagined was replaced by the stress of making ends meet. Once Marissa's talent became apparent, they had raided their savings to help pay for the last four years of lessons and competitions. Brett hadn't been happy about it, but since he was the one who didn't make enough money, Kelly wasn't about to let him complain.

Now it didn't even matter. Going to the next step in gymnastics would take half of their annual income. Brett could never make that much money; without a college degree, he didn't have a lot of options. There would be no traveling to national competitions, no college scholarships, and no chance of training for the Olympics down the road.

Kelly fumed. If God had given Marissa this gift, why wasn't He providing the resources to maximize it? Why couldn't He give her husband a better job?

The dreams we have for marriage and parenthood aren't always fulfilled in the way we envision. And the prayers we offer up for our children aren't always answered in the way we would choose. We start out so hopeful. But when our dreams are battered, so, often, are our hearts.

Maybe you dreamed of being a senior executive, but you can't put in the hours because your husband has to travel for his job, too, and someone needs to be with the kids. Or joining the other families on vacation isn't in the cards this year—again—because your husband's boss cut his bonus. Or the twelve-year-old minivan will have to do for a bit longer.

It's easy to blame our earthly circumstances or the man in our life. *You're not giving me (or our kids) the life I imagined.* It's easy to have turmoil instead of peace.

For a time, Kelly allowed those thoughts to fester. Her marriage suffered. Her husband began to shut down. She shut herself off from God.

Then one day, she watched Brett and Marissa cuddling on the couch, watching TV. She was touched anew by how much they loved each other. And she suddenly realized that God had placed their talented daughter in their family *knowing that they would not have the money to pursue gymnastics at the highest level.*

That meant, by definition, that God had a different purpose for giving Marissa athletic talent. Maybe it was simply to give her something she loved doing!

Similarly, she saw that God had led her and Brett to each other knowing they would not have a lot of worldly resources. Knowing they would have to decide whether they would find joy in each other and be content in all circumstances. Maybe this situation was designed to help them find that contentment . . . if she would let it.

God has placed us in our life circumstances—in this marriage, with these children—for a reason. When our reality doesn't match our expectations, we need to allow God to be God. To show us that His view is bigger than ours. To give us the peace we crave not because we are getting everything we want, but because we are trusting in the One who sees the big picture that we cannot—and who always knows best.

Prayer

Lord, forgive me for thinking I know best. Forgive me for blaming others—or You—when things haven't gone according to my plan. You are the only One who sees the big picture of our lives. You know what we truly need, and it may be different than what I want. Lord, I choose right now to trust You. Help me, day by day, to turn my hopes and expectations over to You, knowing that You love me more than I can imagine, and You always know best. Amen.

Reflect

Do you sometimes feel like you are not getting the life you imagined? Or that your spouse doesn't provide what you started out expecting? Name three things that you are thankful for right now. Throughout the day, express your gratitude to God—and your husband—for the ways your family is provided for today.

NOTES

Day 25

[She] is not afraid of bad news; [her] heart is firm, trusting in the Lord.
Psalm 112:7, ESV

News vs. Truth

After years of dating, business school, high-pressure jobs, and starting a business, Anita had finally found the man of her dreams. Life was good.

But getting married later in life meant the odds of easily having a child were not in her favor.

Trying to get pregnant turned into myriad appointments, which turned into specialists, which turned into genetic counseling, which eventually led to IVF treatments. There were ups . . . and downs. But just when they assumed it would never happen, Anita got pregnant! They were thrilled.

Packages arrived with blankets and toys and equipment from equally thrilled grandparents, and aunts, and uncles. The nursery was full by the time Anita was barely showing.

Then one day at a routine ultrasound appointment, the doctor swept in.

"I have bad news. There's a cyst on the baby's brain, and it indicates chromosomal problems and severe heart issues. The baby won't develop properly and won't go to term. My recommendation is to terminate today, so the pregnancy won't become a risk to you. Is that what you want to do?"

Anita couldn't move. What was happening? Due to her age, they had already gone through all the genetic testing and extra ultrasounds. Everything had been fine! So much so that she had told her husband not to take off work to come to this routine visit.

She numbly left the doctor's office, his words ringing in her ears. *I have bad news. Bad news. Bad news.*

Requests for prayer went out. Anita and her husband were exhausted and overwhelmed, so they decided to take time to think and pray. To do a bit more research. They found a different doctor, one who encouraged more testing and who wouldn't pressure their decision. One test indicated that the cyst might be getting smaller. It wasn't definitive, but it was a tiny glimmer of hope.

Anita longed for God to give her a sign of the direction they should go. She called her best friend from childhood and poured out her heart.

"I don't know what to do! I'm afraid to move forward—afraid to get excited about this baby. There is so much bad news; so many 'what ifs.'"

Her friend smiled into the phone. "What you got is news, Anita. It isn't necessarily truth. I think it's time to step forward and get excited about this baby again. If God has a different decision, then we'll trust Him. But let's get excited."

Anita and her husband were struck by that. They had gotten bad news. But it wasn't necessarily truth. Only God knew the true situation.

And in the meantime, they did know these truths: God had brought them to this place, at this time, with this baby in Anita's womb. Regardless of the outcome, they would receive the blessing of His peace as they followed

His leading. God loved them and asked them to pray fervently for what they longed for—in this case, a healthy baby.

So they did. And a few months later, a perfectly healthy baby boy was born. They wept in thanksgiving—not just that he was healthy, but that he was *there*. The doctor's words had been news, but they weren't truth.

Sisters, let us not readily believe a bad report. Let us grasp one great reason God calls us to not fear: News is not necessarily truth. He is in control. Yes, there will be times when we have to lay down our desires and accept an answer we would not have chosen. But there will also be many times when we see beautiful gifts and miraculous answers that lead to celebration.

Regardless of our circumstances, let us always cling to the greatest truth of all: God is with us. He loves us with an everlasting love. And we can trust Him.

Prayer

Lord, forgive me for so readily believing bad news instead of handing my situation over to You in trust. I do trust You, Jesus. I give You this situation in fervent prayer for the outcome my heart is longing for. I believe; help my unbelief! Help me to turn my fear into celebration of the great truth that You love me, You are there for me, and You are firmly in control. Amen.

Reflect

Think back on your life. What is an example of a time when you got bad news that, in the end, was not truth? Why do we so easily believe bad news, even though we know God is greater than those reports? The next time you get bad news, what is one thing you can do to trust God and set aside fear?

NOTES

Day 26

For you created my inmost being; you knit me together in my mother's womb.
Psalm 139:13

They Aren't You—On Purpose

Kim's husband, Jack, hollered at the TV, supporting his team as he always did. Their teenage son, Joey, was somewhere else during the game, as he usually was, reading or playing video games. It had taken Kim's husband, a gifted athlete, a long time to accept that his son was more into robotics than football. Kim had been pained for years at her husband's feeling that any boy "should" be interested in sports. She was worried her son would grow up feeling inadequate and was grateful when her husband accepted his son for who he was, apologized for pushing him in a direction he was not wired, and cheered on his robotics competitions instead.

So, on this Sunday afternoon, she chuckled at the dynamic. Then it was time to grab her daughter, Bethany, for some mom and daughter bonding time: back-to-school shopping. Things had been a bit tense for months, and this was a way to connect.

"Honey, if we get the school stuff soon, we can get to Macy's before they close. We just have to be back before the Jensens come over for dinner and game night."

Bethany came down the stairs in an old T-shirt, sports shorts, and flip-flops.

Kim sighed, but let it go. While Kim herself always has perfect nails, hair, and clothes, her daughter always said, "That stuff takes too much energy."

As they drove away, Bethany answered Kim's questions in a slightly sullen tone, and Kim started to get annoyed. "What's up with you?"

"I told you I wanted some downtime today, and I've hardly had five minutes to breathe."

"Well," Kim chirped, "You had several hours after church today."

"No, Mom!" Bethany's voice rose. "I had several hours of homework time! I told you I wanted some *downtime*!"

"Well, we're having downtime right now. After Target, we can wander the mall a bit. And then we'll have some downtime tonight with the Jensens."

"That's not downtime!" Kim was shocked to realize there were tears in Bethany's eyes. "Shopping isn't downtime! Time with people isn't downtime! We had that church supper last night, and I had softball all day yesterday and the night before. I've been with people constantly, I'm exhausted, and I need space. I am an INTROVERT, Mom!"

In a flash, Kim's thoughts fell like dominoes. *But it's important to spend time with people and go out and do stuff to recharge!* Her heart sank. *No, it's important for* **me** *to spend time with people to recharge. She's not like me.* Conviction followed. *Oh, no! For years, I've been doing to her what Jack was doing to Joey!*

Tears sprang to her eyes as she apologized to Bethany. Surely her lack of honoring how her daughter was wired was one of the main reasons for the tension between them. She told her daughter she would be praying for God to show her whenever she was inadvertently disrespecting her and gave Bethany permission to tell her that she was "doing it again."

It is so easy to have good intentions and still create a lack of peace with our kids due to wishful thinking or blindness about who they are. Yes, we can provide them with opportunities to explore different avenues and encourage them out of their comfort zones to see if God will grow them in that area. But ultimately, God has created them to be a particular type of "clay," and it is their responsibility (and ours!) to help mold it in beautiful directions . . . not to try to change it entirely.

Our child's gifts and temperament aren't randomly distributed; they're carefully assigned by our Heavenly Father. Let's not just honor them, but honor the One who created them to be the precious people they are.

Prayer

Lord, You have made my child in a particular way, on purpose. If there is any way that You have wired my child that I am missing or even dishonoring, forgive me. Please open my eyes right now to who You want them to be, and make me an instrument to help them become that person—not the person I might be expecting or hoping for. Help me to be a good steward of this precious life You have put into our family. And help my child always know how much I love them. Amen.

Is there a chance that you're missing something important about how your child is wired or making a wrong assumption about them? Do you actively wish that some aspect of your child's personality or nature was different? If so, pray for God to show you how He has wired them. Write down two or three ways you can come alongside them in a way that honors their makeup and helps direct it toward God's best purpose for *them*.

NOTES

Day 27

Be still, and know that I am God.
Psalm 46:10

Maybe There's Something I Can Do!

Raise your hand if you struggle with just a *tiny* desire to control things.

So many of us think we know what is best for our children. And we're going to see that it happens. We try to create the peace that comes from feeling like everything is going the way we want it.

My friend Tina, a mom of five, was usually okay with not trying to control things. But at the start of one school year, that serenity was tested. With teachers having a wide range of personality and experience, many moms fretted over which teacher would be assigned to their kids. Some parents made appointments with the administration to try to ensure the "right" teacher for their child. Others volunteered in the office, hoping to pick up information or lobby for their choice.

But Tina felt she was over all of that. By the time Tina's third son, Liam, entered fifth grade, she felt no need to write notes, lobby, or control things because she knew God was in control. Liam was a sensitive child and needed the right teacher. But she had prayed all summer for God's will and had peace that Liam would get the perfect match: Mrs. Gana. This particular teacher had taught her older son, knew and loved her family, and had won Teacher of the Year. Surely Mrs. Gana would request Liam. All would be well.

Tina confidently logged in on teacher assignment day . . . and froze. Who was Miss Warner? Liam had been assigned a brand-new teacher, someone she had never heard of! *How could this happen, God?!* Why didn't she write that note? Why didn't she do something to make her choice clear? Maybe there was something she could still do!

We all have a decision to make when our plans are tested, our desires are thwarted, or we see the train wreck coming with the school, scout den, or playgroup. Is our first impulse to make that call to a decision-maker? To shoehorn our plan into place? Or is it to stop, take a deep breath, and ask *God* to take control in the midst of a situation we don't totally understand?

Tina is a very high-capacity, strong go-getter. Her first instinct was to charge into the office and "make something happen." If she had, perhaps she could have gotten a different teacher. Or she could have become a tyrant and attempted to control everything the new teacher did with Liam. She could have dwelt on "if only" and sabotaged that year with her doubt and anger.

Instead, in the midst of her panic, she felt the Lord bring her up short. Suddenly, she felt He was challenging her to step back from her initial feelings, take a deep breath, and trust that He had the school year covered. Her mind was flooded with memories of Him being so faithful year after year. Surely this year would be no different. She confessed her sin, swallowed her pride, and waited.

Within weeks, Liam was saying Miss Warner was the best teacher he had ever had. Then, the words that would melt any mom's heart: "I like her because she reminds me of you."

God's plan had been far better than hers.

Ladies, there's nothing wrong with being aware of our children's situation or with trying to head off problems before they start. There's nothing wrong with caring passionately for our kids' well-being. God has put that passion in us! What we have to confront is our subconscious belief that *we* have to be the one moving heaven and earth to get the right outcome to happen. That will never bring peace. Instead, peace comes when we turn it all over to the God of heaven and earth, knowing He is the one who is in control after all.

Prayer

Father, thank You for the gift of my children. Thank You for loving them more than I can ever imagine. Help me to continually let go, give them back to You, and trust in Your ways. Help me to give You control and to hear clearly from You about what, if anything, You are calling me to do. Open my heart to receive Your peace and live out that peace in my family. Amen.

In what area of parenting has God been inviting you to relinquish control? Take a moment to write down your feelings, being honest with God about your hesitation to submit. Do you sense Jesus calling you to a deeper faith and trust in this? How might memorizing a verse like Job 22:21 help you to let go of the reins and let God lead the way?

NOTES

Day 28

You keep him in perfect peace whose mind
is stayed on you, because he trusts in you.
Trust in the LORD forever, for the
LORD GOD is an everlasting rock.
Isaiah 26:3–4, ESV

Keeping Your Mind Stayed on Him

"Do you have a minute?"

I knew in an instant that something was horribly wrong. My closest friend from childhood, Susie, lived in another state, and we weren't able to see each other very often—especially since she and her husband had five active children ranging from age one to fourteen.

I heard her next words, but my brain couldn't make sense of them. "What do you mean, 'He left'?"

Her husband, whom we knew and loved as a wonderful, godly man, had left her for another woman.

Left her. Left their children. Left his faith. Just . . . left.

And my friend was left to start a long, painful journey alone.

Except she never seemed alone. And despite the very real pain, I saw in her an almost impossible level of peace. So much so that I encouraged her to write *When Happily Ever After Shatters,* a book about how she was (and still is) able to get through such a devastating situation with grace.

"How are you doing it?" I would ask, bemused. She shared:

> I watch God showing up, day after day, in not just the big ways, but hundreds of little ones. I think it is sometimes easiest to put the massive fears—like how to feed five kids on a small salary—in God's hands because I can't possibly solve those. But the little fears can get me if I'm not careful. The daily things I think I should be able to handle, like how to fix something that breaks or how to get all the kids to their activities. Those feel more overwhelming sometimes because we don't often think to give those to God. And I believe that's the same for everyone, not just a single mom.

Sisters, we all have challenges. Every journey is different, but every journey shares the common need to trust God and believe that He gives the grace to walk it in faith. Susie has told me that the single parent journey is as joy-filled as any other. Because joy is a choice, and when we make that choice, we can find peace in situations we never thought possible.

How? In Susie's words, "by focusing on Jesus with laser-like intensity." Believing and trusting that even when things are falling apart around us, God will handle our life in His time and His way.

"You keep him in perfect peace whose mind is stayed on you, because he trusts in you."

Perfect peace, God? In such difficult circumstances?

Yes!

God isn't saying that life will be perfect or that all the right circumstances will occur so things *feel* perfect. He isn't saying that things will feel easy. God is saying that despite your very imperfect circumstances, despite the hard things that come, despite your fears, frustrations, and failures, He *will* give you perfect peace as you focus on Him and not on the circumstances around you.

This isn't the fleeting peace of a car that works well, a house without major issues, a happy child, a healthy body, a balanced checkbook, a paid-off credit card, or a quiet moment. Jesus says He doesn't give us peace like the world does. His peace does not rely on our circumstances, and it does not come and go. It remains a steady offering. A quiet place in the storm.

When life is anything but peaceful, God says He is our peace. When our hearts are anxious, God says He will give us peace at all times and in every way. When our minds are overwhelmed with worry, God says, *Keep your mind on Me, and I will give you* perfect *peace.*

His perfect peace passes all understanding because it simply doesn't make sense. It shouldn't be, but it is.

Prayer

Lord, it is so easy to focus on those big worries, and even easier to focus on the little ones. And yet You tell me to place my thoughts firmly, permanently, on You. Lord, I want to have my mind stayed on You. I want to trust You forever. Please forgive me when my trust falters and I focus on my circumstances. I believe that You are the everlasting Rock. Help me to focus on You with a laser-like intensity and receive the peace and joy You promise, no matter what is going on around me. Amen.

Is there a circumstance or trial that is creating a lack of peace in your life right now? What would it mean to have your "mind stayed on God" in the midst of that? Consider two or three ways you can do that in the weeks ahead. Then journal what happens as a result.

NOTES

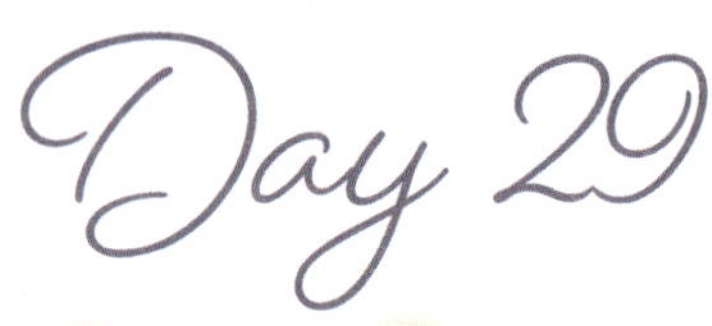

I will not offer burnt offerings to the
Lord my God that cost me nothing.
2 Samuel 24:24, ESV

Friendship That Costs Something

The folks who lived in "The Circle"—a circular street of fifteen homes—had become casual friends over the years. They had backyard barbeques, jointly watched rival college football games, and cheered on the local high school teams. They argued about politics and traded local gossip. Jasmine, Julie, their husbands, and several other families in the group were followers of Christ who invited the others to church, with mixed results.

Jasmine and Julie enjoyed these gatherings, but they had busy kids and opposite work schedules, so they rarely spent deeper time together. Their friendship, like all the neighbor relationships, was surface-level and undemanding. They were busy, but lonely.

That all changed the night that Millie, a single mom in the group, suddenly burst into tears. She was pregnant, she sobbed, and the father was no longer in the picture. She felt shame and despair and didn't know what to do.

As her neighbors gathered around her, she blurted out that she was considering abortion. She looked to see if they were shocked or disappointed. Instead, Jasmine, Julie, and several of the other women hugged her. They encouraged her to look into adoption. And they committed to praying for her and the baby.

The next week at a potluck, Millie said that she didn't want to end her pregnancy, but felt she had no other choice. She wanted the baby, but could see no way to manage another child. An abortion seemed easier than the pain of losing her baby to another couple.

Jasmine and Julie huddled with the other neighbors, then came back to Millie. If she decided to have this baby, they committed to rolling up their sleeves and to help her. They would walk alongside her and the kids for the long haul.

Millie was stunned. She promised to think about it. But then an ultrasound revealed the presence of not just one, but two babies. Twins!

How serious were Millie's neighbors about helping her? Twins were going to be a lot of work. But by now she couldn't bear the thought of losing them. After taking a big gulp, Jasmine, Julie, their families, and several other neighbors assured her that they meant it. They would be there.

Several months later, Millie gave birth to two precious babies. When she started back to work, Jasmine, Julie, and a few others started a rotating childcare calendar; each took at least one day a week where they would babysit the twins and help her nine-year-old son with his homework. Other friends provided dinner; still others helped with bills when her funds were low.

As they worked together to help Millie, Jasmine and Julie became very close. They were no longer in an undemanding acquaintanceship but bound together as sisters in Christ. They were no longer consumed with the trivia of politics, but with an investment of eternal worth. They were exhausted, but they were truly enjoying life. Because their hearts were full.

When King David was enduring a painful time of separation from the Lord, he was instructed to build an altar to the Lord in a specific spot. The owner of the property tried to give him the land for free, but David insisted on paying for it. He refused to offer to God that which cost him nothing.

It is so easy to be buried in the chaos of the moment and feel isolated and lonely. We want friendships to just come our way, to magically fit in between all the other things that take our time.

Are we willing to extend ourselves when it's inconvenient or expensive? Are we willing to give of ourselves in a sweet sacrifice to God? Do we engage in authentic community that costs us something? That is where the real friendships—God's great blessing for our lives—are found.

Prayer

Lord, forgive me for becoming so consumed with the little trivial pursuits that don't matter, that I miss what does. Forgive me for wishing I had more friends, or more time with friends, and not realizing that having that will probably cost me something. I know that when I invest in others, I will gain far more than I give. Jesus, I am so grateful that is the way You work. Help me to see and reach out to those You want me to bless. I pray that You would take this time and create wonderful friendships from it. Amen.

If you are honest with yourself, are you wishing for richer friendships, but wanting them to just magically appear? How might investing in the lives of others give you the opportunity for true, eternal, life-giving relationships? Write down a few ways you might do that.

NOTES

Day 30

Let us hold fast the confession of our hope without wavering, for He who promised is faithful.
Hebrews 10:23, NKJV

Divine Planning

Although I knew that time with kids goes fast, I rarely thought about the time when our kids would graduate and move on. That is, until my daughter started her junior year of high school. I was juggling her volleyball tournaments and flying off to speaking engagements as usual when my long-time speaking agent began to get inquiries for me to speak the next fall. I idly thought, *Hmm, that is Morgen's senior year.*

Wait!! Morgen's senior year?!

With perfect clarity, I saw that my "mommy-daughter" days with her were numbered. And I wanted to be there for *all* the important moments of her senior year.

But how did I know when those moments would be? I have to accept speaking engagements months or years in advance. I could block out obvious dates like prom or the volleyball championship. But the truly priceless moments are never scheduled. I already wrestled with the usual working-mom guilt of inevitably missing some of them. But this was *SENIOR YEAR*. I didn't want to miss any of them!

And I couldn't just turn down all my speaking invitations. For me and Jeff, not only is this a vital ministry to relationships, but our full-time income comes from writing, speaking, and crucial secondary sources such as selling books at events. How could I know exactly which events to decline in order to be home one year from now on the exact dates I would *need* to be home? And somehow still pay staff salaries?

I couldn't. I felt God nudging me to step back and trust Him.

"Father," I prayed, "I don't want to miss the important moments next year. Only you know when those will be. I don't have the courage to turn down the revenue from these events. So if there's a particular day that you know I would miss something important, just don't let that invitation come in in the first place."

Well, God heard my prayer. The usual rate of speaking queries dropped dramatically. Occasionally, when I panicked, my agent just chuckled, "Remember? You prayed for this."

My daughter's senior year was a time of great ups and downs. And I was there. I was there to help her think through all her college essays. To encourage her final attempts at the SAT. For most of her all-day volleyball tournaments. And I was there to help my competitive daughter, who had played in every game for six years, wrestle through the heartbreak of being permanently benched, halfway through the season, in favor of a much taller player. I was there to help her navigate friendships and shop for dorm goodies. And I was there to watch her apprehensively click a link on college admission day and explode with excitement. What a sweet, special year it was!

Money had, of course, been much tighter. For the first time, we had to temporarily dip into our line of credit to pay salaries. So, in August, after moving Morgen to college, I asked our bookkeeper just how much our speaking revenue had dropped the previous year.

"Actually," she said, "Even though the *number* of speaking engagements was way down, making your secondary book sales go way down, your actual speaking income was a little higher!"

My mouth dropped open. How could it be?

But Jeff and I knew how it could be. Our big, rich, faithful God was making a point: *You can trust me. You can trust that I reduced the number of engagements, but made it up by giving you more speaking income at each one. So you can trust me with the downturn in your secondary income, too.*

Sisters, all God asks is our obedience to His callings—most especially as a mom and, if we're married, as a wife. He has an unlimited supply, and we can trust Him when we set our hearts toward the things He prioritizes.

Prayer

Lord, it can be so scary to say no to something, to prioritize something else. But I know You call me to that. Help me to see what Your priorities are for me. Give me clarity on what You are calling me to do, and then the courage to do it. Help me to trust and not second-guess. And bless the special times with my family in the process. Amen.

In what area might God be calling You to sacrifice for something more important? What is it that you need to prioritize? What do you need to say no to? What fears are preventing you from moving forward? Spend some time journaling about this, pray about it, and be willing to act as God leads.

NOTES

Dear friend, I hope all is well with you and that you are as healthy in body as you are strong in spirit.

3 John 2, NLT

Take Care

After a few minutes of chitchat after church, Lisa and her friend Tracy were headed in opposite directions to pick up their kids from Sunday school. With a quick hug, Tracy said, "Love you, Lisa. Take care!"

That evening, as Lisa scanned her calendar, the phrase came back to her: *Take care!* And she thought, *Nope, no time for that this week!* Between work, errands, planning the lesson for her women's small group, the kids' sports practices and homework, getting dinner on the table, cleaning up, and spending a few minutes processing the day with her husband before they both fell asleep, there was no time to *take care* . . . or do anything else for herself.

As busy moms we can feel caught between a rock and a hard place. Downtime is hard to find to begin with. And if we do, we can feel selfish about taking time and attention away from other priorities. Yet we also know that if we don't practice at least *some* level of self-care, we're not going to be in any condition to manage our lives and love our people well.

As the saying goes, "You can't pour from an empty cup."

The next day, after her college freshman daughter caught yet another cold,

Tracy overheard her husband giving her a bit of a talking-to about constantly staying up all night and eating too much junk food. "Your immune system is fried," he said. "You need to learn how to take care of yourself."

Tracy was suddenly reminded that if an earthly father cares about his daughter's wellness, our Heavenly Father cares for us far more. In Psalm 23, the shepherd tends to the sheep by making sure they're rested and watered. When Elijah is weary from his long journey, an angel provides food so he can renew his strength. And when the disciples are so busy that they don't have a chance to eat, Jesus draws them away from the crowds for rest and replenishment.

Tracy realized: God does not want His people to get worn out and rundown! And He provides practical ways for us to be replenished and nourished. But we have to listen. We have to accept it.

Sisters, we know all this, don't we? We know that caring for our body, mind, and spirit with healthy nutrition, physical activity, rest, friendships, devotions, and recreation can have powerful results: more energy, a better mood and outlook, more effective stress management, and godly motivations. We know that taking care of ourselves *now* provides the foundation for a healthy *future* with our family for years to come. We also know that it provides a great example for them to follow.

If we're honest, we know it. We just have to act on it. For if we don't, we are often working *against* what God is trying to do to care for us in answer to our own desperate prayers!

Tracy called Lisa that night. To fit some self-care into their busy lives, they decided to team up. They put their youngest kids in a Moms Morning Out program so they could have a few precious free hours and began walking together three days a week, talking, praying, and encouraging one another as they walked. Being out in God's creation nourished their spirits, and their minds were sharper to face their demanding days. They slept better at night. And they developed a close friendship. Very soon, their families benefited from happier, more peaceful, and more patient moms.

As we step out in this area, we will find that investing only a few hours a week into simple acts of self-care will give us so much more.

Prayer

Lord, I'm so grateful You created me and You know me inside and out. You created me with a need for rest, sleep, good fuel to keep me healthy, and movement to keep my body strong. Lord, forgive me for the many times I have told my kids they need to eat well and live well, and yet I failed to do the same. It can feel so hard, when there are so many demands on my time. But I know You will be putting opportunities in front of me. Help me to see and accept them as straight from Your loving hand. Amen.

Reflect

Do you feel guilty about taking time to care for yourself? Do you feel you don't have time? Think about how God cares for every aspect of our lives, minds, and bodies. What is one thing you can begin to do today to improve your well-being? Commit to that step, knowing that it will impact not just you, but everyone around you in a positive way.

NOTES

Day 32

What is that to you? You follow Me.
John 21:22, NKJV

Helium Hand

"I have a proposal for you," said the church leader to my friend Donna, "and it's right up your alley." She explained that one of the kids in the congregation had become homeless and needed a loving home for the rest of the school year. "We know you welcome the kids in the neighborhood," the leader continued. "Your house is a revolving door of hospitality. Would you pray about housing this sweet child?"

Donna's thoughts raced ahead. Her oldest had just left for college, so there was that spare bedroom available. She loved being able to serve others. And now this respected leader was directly asking her to meet an important need. Donna promised to give a quick answer and raced home to talk to her husband, Brad. He listened quietly.

Then he said, "Honey . . . I hope you didn't have 'helium hand.' Please tell me you didn't raise your hand and say, 'Sure, we'll do it!'"

"But honey!" Donna protested. "The need is so great, and we have the resources to meet it!"

"Yes," Brad answered slowly, "but . . . I don't know whether this feels right. I just don't know."

All of Donna's assumptions about moving forward screeched to an unexpected halt. They couldn't do it if Brad didn't have peace about it.

Maybe you've been in similar situations. A clear need arises, and you quickly jump into the fray. Or maybe you're that capable person to whom leaders come for just about everything. After all, the saying goes, "If you want a job done, give it to a busy person." All of us seem to have that tendency to take on the world—not just our own corner of it, but any corner that needs a touch of our talent or heart.

Yet that doesn't mean God wants us to do it.

How often have we jumped to act without pausing to be sure that God has given us peace that *we* are the one who is supposed to do so?

I once heard this great advice for wives to pause the tendency to take over when their husband doesn't do something fast enough, but it could apply to anyone: "Don't knee-jerk to make things happen. Wait. Give God time to bring an answer His way."

Our calling isn't to figure out how to accomplish something; it is to figure out what God wants us to do—and not do—and to obey. Especially when we're tempted by pressure from or about others.

Two thousand years ago, Jesus talked to Peter about what God would accomplish in his life. But Peter wanted the bigger picture: What would happen to the other disciples? Jesus answered, "What is that to you? You follow me."

Two thousand years later, my friends paused and prayed. What would "following Him" look like here? Donna had to respect her husband's continuing unease. She told the leader no, quailing at the disappointed look in her eyes.

But soon another family stepped forward. God had been tugging on their hearts to take this child, they said. They couldn't get away from it. They just *knew* that this was an assignment for them, and they wouldn't have peace until they accepted.

Donna realized that she could have taken in this boy out of all good intentions, despite a lack of peace, and not only would she have brought a literal lack of peace to her family and marriage, she would have denied both the boy and the other family the blessing that God intended for them!

Oh, the peace that comes when we look for *only* and *exactly* what God has put into *our* hands to do. What is it to us what other people might say or do? "You follow Me."

Prayer

Father, when a need arises, it's hard to set aside the pressure to please someone else or follow what I think seems right. Guard me from the impulse to jump to answer the need in front of me, and instead, help me to answer Your call. To discover what You would have me do and to do it. Help me to pause and listen for Your voice over what other people think. I desire to follow You. Amen.

Reflect

Have you ever jumped in to tackle something despite feeling a lack of peace about it? What happened? Similarly, consider a time when you knew God *did* give you peace about doing something, even if it was challenging or hard. What happened as a result? What is one lesson you've learned about how to avoid "helium hand"?

NOTES

For I long to see you, that I may impart to you some spiritual gift to strengthen you—that is, that we may be mutually encouraged by each other's faith, both yours and mine.

Romans 1:11–12, ESV

Prioritizing the People

On an afternoon like many others, a mom sinks wearily onto the playground bench for a moment of rest while her little girl runs and plays. Maybe the melodic "ding" causes her to pull out her phone, or perhaps it's just an automatic reflex to reach for it in unoccupied moments. Maybe she's been longing for an opportunity to zone out from the stresses of the day and be entertained just for a quick minute. But that "quick minute" turns into five, then ten, then thirty.

At first she just checks her notifications, catches up with friends on social media, and messages her sister about lunch plans. But soon she's clicking through news articles from online acquaintances about the latest problems with politics, then local news, then church drama. And a search for dinner recipes becomes a Pinterest trap.

Wow, look at Tara Smith's new table settings!

I have no idea who MomRocks212 is, but how does she come up with such great recipes and manage all those kids at the same time?

A familiar sound breaks into her awareness—the patter of a certain four-year-old's feet—and suddenly her daughter's face is inches from hers. "Didn't you hear me, Mommy? Come swing me, I want you to swing me!"

And the thought occurs to her: *When did scrolling through pictures of other people's lives become more important than living my own?*

It's an easy trap, and one reason we often feel an underlying emptiness or agitation instead of an underlying peace. Whatever social media we log on to or whatever news sources we read, the feed is never going to end. There's always more out there. A quick check-in easily turns into a marathon as we try not to miss anything.

But what exactly is it that we don't want to miss?

A friend once told me that it's not technology she loves, it's the people on the other end. There's nothing wrong with technology; the question is whether we are using it primarily to further the real-life connections, fellowship, and growth that God has for us. And if we're honest, that's often not the goal. We lose ourselves in the social media feed of news organizations, celebrities, and "friends" we hardly know. We miss out on life with our kids, husband, or friends while we are head down to our smartphones. And how many of us have secretly felt better that we can message a friend as a substitute for *truly* catching up and hearing what is going on in her life?

Now, don't get me wrong: There is no way we can fully invest in deep, meaningful, time-intensive friendships with every person we know. With some, we have to settle for updates that only skim the surface. And frankly, as one who is often out of town speaking, I am *grateful* technology allows me to stay in some sort of touch with those I can't see very often.

My problem—our problem—is that we too often mistake surfacy updates for real connection. Could we have used that fifteen minutes to call a friend instead of scrolling through images from people we hardly know and news about people we definitely don't know?

Calling that friend takes a bit of effort. Pulling ourselves out of our technology break after five minutes to push our child on the swing takes effort. It is easier to scroll.

Sisters, when Jesus walked the earth, He clearly prioritized fellowship and connection. He was never distracted. He attended to those around Him. Today, God has precious fellowship for us. Real relationships. With family. With friends. Yes, sometimes that will be done through technology, but let us ensure that technology is being used to *build* meaningful relationships, not avoid them.

Prayer

Lord, forgive me for the ways I've been lazy. For how I'm so willing to keep scrolling on my smartphone and miss the beautiful real life and relationships You've put in front of me. Lord, bring to my mind now those people You intend to be a greater part of my life—those whom I can encourage and be encouraged by. In those times when I am at risk of mindlessly scrolling, bring me up short when You want me to connect with someone instead. Help me to attend to those around me the way You want me to. Amen.

Reflect

Take a moment to honestly consider: Is connecting with technology causing you to miss out on real relationships that are more important? Write down two or three people that you feel you should probably connect with IRL (in real life) and how you will do so.

NOTES

Day 34

The path of the righteous is like the light of dawn,
which shines brighter and brighter until full day.
Proverbs 4:18, ESV

Walking the Path with Your Child

"Mom, the sheriff wants to talk to you."

Jessica could hear the quiver in her daughter's voice. It matched the one in her heart.

The sheriff came on. "Mrs. Johnson, I have Kayla with me. She's intoxicated and vomiting. I know it is a long drive, but I need you to come and get her."

Jessica's mind raced as she scrambled to get her things together and break the news to her husband, the church pastor. Their daughter had never done anything like this before!

Seventeen-year-old Kayla had been invited to a country music festival two hours away. She was going with a new friend from church—a friend from a nice, respectable family whose dad worked in the sheriff's department. How much safer could it be? And since Kayla had responsibly attended the same concert the year before and was generally mature and respectful of rules, Jessica felt fine about letting her go again. Now, blame, shame, fear, and anger raced through her mind.

On the way home, the story tumbled out. The church friend had gotten alcohol, planning to party while they were away from home. Kayla found herself in a new situation with new friends and the opportunity to experiment with something she had never tried before. Since Kayla hadn't eaten much, it only took a few shots for her to become completely drunk. Soon, her friends had abandoned her, and she was sick as a dog and sitting in the sheriff's office—hungover and ashamed—while her mom wondered what on earth to do.

Many of us can relate. Sometimes our kids act the opposite of how they were raised. Maybe they succumbed to peer pressure, took the wrong path, and our heart is broken. Or maybe we look at their personality or their friends and worry that it is just a matter of time.

The thing is: Every child's path to the top of the mountain looks different. It will certainly be easier for them if they stay on the narrow way; if they hold to God's precepts; if they don't fall off the edge and get bruised on the rocks below. But if they do, God will use it.

Sisters, we equip our kids with the best backpacks and equipment we can. We show them that narrow path and encourage them to the top. But we can't carry their backpack for them. We can't make them take the right road. They will choose where they step and which paths to take. Some people take straight paths to the top, while others meander in and out of the valley and fog, and some tumble down into the rocks for a time.

When they do, they need us to stop thinking about ourselves and our embarrassment and just join them where they are. They usually know they have made mistakes, and they need to see the unconditional love of the Father reflected in their earthly parents. They need us to say, "I know this is hard. But I love you, and I'm here for you through all of it."

Jessica told me that by God's grace that is what they were able to do. Both girls got a citation on their record. Both had to pay fines, repair relationships, and earn back trust. But both received love and forgiveness. And their parents thanked God their girls had experienced a "soft fall" and seen the consequences of their rebellious behavior early, rather than having a much harder fall down the road.

It is hard to watch our little hikers head in wrong directions. But we can trust them to our great big God, knowing that He hates the broken times even more than we do, and that He will use those difficult times for their growth as they eventually climb to the top.

Prayer

Lord, I pray You would give me Your unconditional love. When my child goes against everything I've tried to tell them, it almost feels better to withhold affection or make my child feel guilty. And yet, You don't do that with me. You expect me to follow You, and You convict me of my wrongdoing, but You are right there with me in my mistakes, loving me. Thank You for that, Lord. Help me to love my child that same way and entrust the outcome to You. Amen.

Is there a way that your child is not acting as you have raised them to? Does it cause not only concern for them, but embarrassment and other self-focused feelings for you? How can you set aside those feelings and show your child unconditional love in the journey?

NOTES

Day 35

You rule over the surging sea;
when its waves mount up, you still them.
Psalm 89:9

Life Beyond the Breakers

It had been a rough summer. I'd been trying to keep all the plates spinning in a season with great demands on my time as a parent, as a wife, as a ministry leader. I had gotten snippy with my kids many times because they weren't moving fast enough or being cooperative enough.

Of course, snapping at our kids always results in them doing exactly what we want, right?

No matter how I tried—and oh, I tried—I couldn't make everything work. Every day brought a different challenge. I was stressed. Peace was nowhere in sight.

One long weekend in September, some friends invited us to their beach house. It was such a blessing to just sit and read, walk along the beach, and run around in the surf with our family. I love boogie boarding and playing in the waves. Except this weekend the waves were much stronger than usual. I kept getting knocked down. Just as I would get my bearings and begin to stand, another wave would come crashing in, tumbling me around until I came up gasping for air.

I'm supposed to be on vacation, I thought, almost snapping at God. *Forget it.*

My family and friends were calling to me to join them out further, but I said no way. If I was getting whomped like this in the shallows, why would I go deeper, where I had no footing? I gave up, retreated, and sat on the beach feeling annoyed and sorry for myself.

Soon afterwards, I described my experience to a friend. She said the exact same thing had happened to her. But she finally ventured past the unusually large breakers and discovered the deeper waters were strong but much more gentle. The powerful currents were there, but they swelled below the surface. She could ride the waves up to their peaks and back down to the troughs, then watch from afar as they hit the beach shelf, rose up, and crashed against the shoreline.

She loved it. Once she got over the fear of being far from shore, it was so peaceful.

She realized that in order to experience peace in the waves, we have to be willing to let go of what we think of as certain footing. We must give up the illusion that we can control things in the shallows and stop clinging to the shoreline. We must have the courage to go where the water is deeper and simply let ourselves be carried.

We women tend to be really, really good at trying to "make things work." We are really good at keeping the plates spinning. We like to feel that things are in control. But I almost wonder if God sometimes allows so many waves at once to point out, *My child, you need to realize you aren't really in control anyway. I don't want you to get knocked down with every wave that comes along. Let go. Come to the deeper waters. Trust Me. Let Me carry you.*

Sisters, those deeper waters can be scary, can't they? In the shallows we still have the illusion of control. That illusion goes away when we swim out to the deeper places. We don't know what is under the water. The shore can look farther away than we would like. We can't stand; we can only be carried.

But that's where Jesus asks us to live our whole life. Beyond those breakers, in a place where we feel His power carrying us over and through the challenges, rather than getting destroyed by them.

Instead of clinging to the shoreline, let's cling to Him.

Lord, I confess that I want to be in control because it feels safer. But I know it is not. I know that the only true security is found in You. Jesus, please give me the courage to let go and venture out beyond where I can stand, beyond where I have the illusion of control, into the deeper waters with You. Lord, I want You to carry me. During times of fear, reassure me. Help me to not try to swim back to the shallows and instead see, every day, that You are moving in ways far greater than I could. And that I can trust You. Amen.

Reflect

What are the "waves" in your life? Something related to your marriage, your kids, your job? Are there ways you find yourself "clinging to the shoreline," fighting those waves and trying to make things work, only to be knocked down over and over? What would it look like to move beyond your comfort zone and let Jesus carry you instead of trying to control those things?

NOTES

Day 36

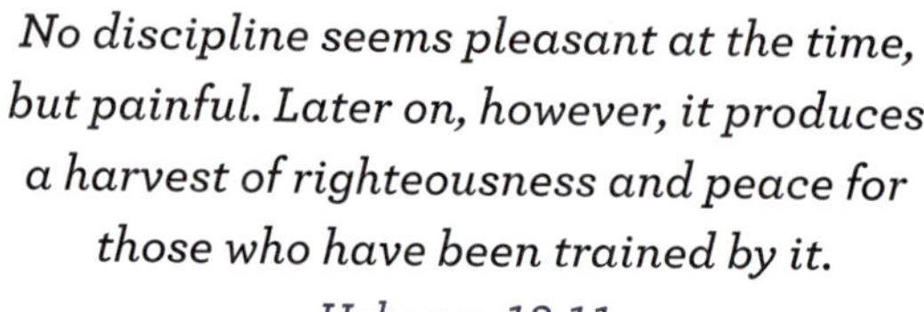

No discipline seems pleasant at the time, but painful. Later on, however, it produces a harvest of righteousness and peace for those who have been trained by it.

Hebrews 12:11

Current Pains for Later Gains

When our daughter was almost a year old, she developed the habit of twisting her hair. It was cute for about a minute—until she started pulling her hair out. We realized that when she was anxious or upset, she would reach up and wind her little fingers in her hair and pull. She was using hair pulling like other babies used a pacifier.

For six months, we gently pulled her hand down each time she started twisting. We tried distraction techniques. We substituted other stringy things to keep her hands occupied. Nothing worked. She grew more and more upset, and we grew more and more concerned about how this condition would affect her future.

Finally, a professional suggested that we shave her head.

What? Shave the beautiful blonde hair off our beautiful eighteen-month-old little girl? What kind of parents did that?

Turns out, the kind of parents who are willing to endure short-term pain for long-term gain.

After we cut our daughter's hair to half an inch long—too short for her little fingers to grasp—there were constant tears and frustrated outbursts from her. It was heartbreaking to see her not know how to cope with anxiety or calm herself down. Sometimes we received judgmental or pitying looks from strangers. But we knew we had to remove the focus of her unhealthy habit in order to break it altogether. We hoped an uncomfortable decision now would lead to freedom later.

Around the same time, a friend's middle school son discovered that marijuana calmed his anxiety. Soon he became emotionally addicted, and his life spiraled dreadfully downhill. A counselor advised his parents to remove him from temptation by providing him with "new playgrounds and new playmates." The parents withdrew him from his school for a season.

As you can imagine, the son was enraged. He told his parents that he hated them. He tried to run away. They were terrified he would get hurt, but even more terrified they would lose him to drugs. They stood their ground.

In both cases, these children had to endure the discomfort we, as parents, willingly placed on them. And in being the "bad guy," we had to endure our children's pain and lack of understanding. But it was so needed—and so worth it. Within two or three years without the ability to act on their temptations, our daughter outgrew the hair-pulling habit and our friends' son overcame his addiction to marijuana.

Sisters, I wonder if we need to learn this lesson for ourselves. Is there anything we enjoy doing that honestly isn't healthy? That just feeds our anxiety? If so, we need to be our own bad guy and identify what pleasurable habits we must break now for the sake of a more healthy, joyful life later. Do we secretly enjoy watching news commentators agitatedly yell at each other on cable shows, only to feel more agitated ourselves? Are we indulging in negative one-upmanship with our girlfriends ("Oh, what your husband did is nothing! Listen to this idiotic thing Jason did yesterday"), only to feel dissatisfied in our marriage? Do we "feel better" if we tell our husband how to handle every five minutes with the kids while we're out, only to realize that our husband is angry at our lack of trust . . . and we really don't feel better at all?

Maybe it's time to make some changes—and be glad we did.

My prayer is that we would do for ourselves what we do for our children: enforce the courageous hard work to change unhealthy, anxiety-creating habits now in order to reap joy and peace for the long term.

Prayer

Lord, if I am honest with myself, I have known in my heart that this habit was unhealthy. You have tried to get my attention, You have pricked my conscience, and You have shown me that it was leading me down a bad path. And yet I wanted to do this thing more than I wanted to listen to You—even if following You would reap greater rewards in the long run. Lord, forgive me. Right now, I ask that You would show me exactly what change You are calling me to make and give me the strength to make it. I trust in You, God. And I look forward with hope to the peace that will come as a result. Amen.

List three seemingly minor things that you do that are probably responsible for causing angst, frustration, or anxiety in your life. Next to each one, list what you could do to give up that behavior or change that habit. Then pick at least one to start with and commit to that change—perhaps with the support of an accountability partner. Journal what happens.

NOTES

Day 37

Who of you by worrying can add a single hour to your life?
Since you cannot do this very little thing,
why do you worry about the rest?
Luke 12:25–26

Possibilities Aren't Realities

Alia chased after a half-dressed toddler as he scampered around the house trying to escape a diaper change. But her mind was elsewhere. She slowly walked into the bathroom, her heart pounding—and not in a good way. The test had finished processing and the bright pink line was as clear as day: She was pregnant.

She and Dan had planned for it. She knew it was a huge blessing. But instead of feeling happy, she felt dread. Instead of excitement, anxiety flared.

A few years back, Alia and Dan had it all figured out. They started trying to have children just a few weeks after the wedding—and would have started on their honeymoon if her husband had anything to say about it! They both wanted children desperately, and when better to start?

With her first positive pregnancy test, Alia was filled with excitement. But it quickly turned to fear when the bleeding began. Her doctor confirmed she was miscarrying but dismissed her concerns, saying these things happen.

The grief hit hard. Learning that miscarriages were fairly common should have brought some comfort. But somehow it still felt like a personal failure that she lost her very first baby. Every pregnant woman she saw felt like a personal attack. And as she thought about getting pregnant again, fear took hold.

When she did become pregnant, she couldn't relax. Every day, she waited for another miscarriage to begin. What happened before could happen again. She knew the stats. It was hard to not constantly imagine worst-case scenarios.

It wasn't until halfway through her pregnancy that she finally allowed herself to relax and believe that she would have a healthy baby. And at forty weeks, their son was born. What a joy he was!

A year later, Alia and Dan started seriously discussing having a second baby. Alia wanted a large family but didn't want months of fear and anxiety. What if she miscarried again?

That was her mindset the day she saw the bright pink line. The moment was one of anxiety instead of joy.

Whether it's over a pregnancy, our child's safety, our marriage, or any other concern, when we allow anxiety to fester, we lose our sense of reality. Possibilities become exaggerated and appear etched in stone. The equilibrium that should live in the heart of every believer seems to disappear. And losing our way can feel like losing everything.

It can also hold us back from great blessings.

A few days after seeing that bright pink line, Alia watched her firstborn son running around. And her mind turned to another firstborn Son. He had come to this earth, had lived and died for her, *that she would have abundant life*. Not a life of fear. Not a life spent holding back to protect her feelings. Instead, He commanded her to trust Him and not worry about tomorrow.

Alia saw that Jesus wanted her to have *joy* in her pregnancies. She knew she had to force herself to release her worry to God. Sometimes that involved praying that He would take the burden of her stress and anxiety, and other days it meant thanking God for the blessings of the pregnancy journey—even with the potential unknowns ahead.

Jesus knows what it feels like to face fear. And His solution is for us to resolutely remember that giving in to fear will accomplish nothing, that He cares for us and provides for all our needs.

It is understandable that our minds might be tempted to flash back to our worries. It is understandable that we might be tempted to numb ourselves to protect our feelings. But God knows those are traps. He wants us to never lose the joy of the journey in front of us.

Prayer

Lord, I know that under my chronic area of worry is a lack of trust. Forgive me that it feels risky to trust You, the Creator of the universe. I know how crazy that is. Lord, help me to believe that You really do care about me more than about the birds of the air that You feed or the flowers that You clothe. Help me remember that You love me so much that You came and lived and died for me. I tell You, Lord, that I want to lay my fears at Your feet and never pick them up again. Help me to live a life of peace instead of fear. Amen.

Demolish Anxiety-Causing Thoughts/Actions

Is there an area of such concern in your life that you find yourself either worrying regularly or holding back from delight and enjoyment in order to protect your feelings? What would it look like if you truly set every worry aside? What would it look like to not hold back? If doing so feels risky, why?

NOTES

Day 38

See what great love the Father has lavished on us, that we should be called children of God!
1 John 3:1

Who Am I Now?

Would she dare? Could she do it? What if she failed? Lorena decided to go for it. After years of taking the kids to piano lessons, reminding them to practice, and feeling nervous and proud at their recitals, it was her turn. She would have weekly lessons and practice time. She was excited, but she also battled the voice of self-doubt.

The doubt had seeped in as her children left home, one by one.

When they began having children, she and her husband had jointly decided that she would stay home. Despite the financial sacrifices their decision required, she had never regretted it. A competitive pianist in her younger years, Lorena had to set aside lessons and competitions. She did it willingly because she loved having the time to invest fully into the lives of her children and their friends.

But when her last child was leaving for college, that little voice of self-doubt burst to the front of her consciousness: *Who am I now?*

Of course, she was still a mom: once a mom, always a mom. But the role of a mom changes. After all, for years our job as mothers is all-encompassing—we're nurses, counselors, recreation directors, tutors, chefs, chauffeurs, financial managers, and about 100 other things. Yet at each stage, we slowly let go of our children. We go from being a director and enforcer to being a voice of guidance and advice.

We still think, "Mom knows best," but at some point, we're not that type of mom anymore.

Who am I now?

Suddenly, our hours are freed up—hours in which we can do other things. But what do we even want to do? If we are married, we have hours more to spend with our husband, but is there some rebuilding to be done? If we want to work a different job—one that isn't constrained by time we used to need for our kids—what might it look like? Or if we want to start an outside job for the first time, does what we've done and learned as a mom really matter?

If we rely on earthly measures of success—income, status, position—we might doubt the value and relevance of our responsibilities as moms, especially as they begin to wind down. But as children of God, those earthly cues are irrelevant.

Who am I now? I am a child of God. I'm a child of the King of all creation. And that will never change. Our amazing, awesome, eternal identity transcends any earthly role.

Friends, seasons will pass. Whether you're a brand-new mom or a grandmother, your responsibilities will change. But your identity in Christ is unmoving and unchanging. Once we have accepted Jesus, *that* is who we are. All along the pathways of our lives, God knows us, loves us, and has plans for us, His children.

As for Lorena, the mom who started taking piano lessons? She found herself saying not only, "I can do this!" but also, "I've still got it!"

She thrived as new and old facets of her personality began to shine. She discovered new strengths. After playing in her first recital, she realized that her long-ago capacity for taking risks was still intact. Her unique sparkle and what she valued hadn't faded or gotten lost in the shuffle. Her willingness to try something new carried her to new places, and that gave her the courage to spread her wings even more.

In every endeavor, who am I? I am a child of God.

Prayer

Lord, help me see that ultimately, whether I'm deep in the most intense season of motherhood or an empty nester, I am not primarily a mom; I'm primarily Your daughter. You have given me skills and capabilities as a mother, but also in other things. Thank You for those gifts and those purposes. Help me to see what You have for me in every season, and to know when and how to pursue it. Amen.

Has your self-image changed in your journey as a mom? Do you find yourself questioning whether the world values what you have to offer or whether you can be successful doing new things? What has God built into you as a unique individual that you may not have had the time or capacity to pursue? Now or in the future, what endeavor might God want you to take on beyond that of being a mom?

NOTES

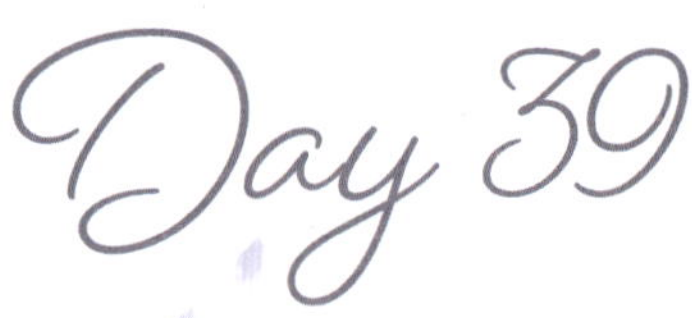

My heart rejoices in the LORD*! . . . The* LORD *makes some poor and others rich; he brings some down and lifts others up. . . . For all the earth is the* LORD*'s, and he has set the world in order.*

1 Samuel 2:1, 7–8, NLT

How Do We Respond to His Decision for Us?

She was the first lady of creation. Eve had everything: a strong husband, every privilege, and a close relationship with God. But then God told her and Adam His decision for them: They could eat of any tree except *this one*. And Eve started obsessing over this one thing she felt God was keeping from her. She allowed the enemy to whisper in her ear. Eve took her eyes off of God's many blessings, doubted His goodness, and chose to walk away.

Many years down the road, a different woman had a choice to make. Hannah was barren for years—and relentlessly ridiculed for it. But she kept her heart soft. She persisted in prayer, believing the desire of her heart aligned with God's best for her. She promised the Lord that if He answered her prayer, she would dedicate her son back to Him. When she learned of God's decision and Samuel was born, she praised God. But surprisingly, she made no mention of her much-prayed-for son. Instead, she focused solely on worshiping her King.

> *"My heart rejoices in the* Lord*! . . . There is no one holy like the* Lord*; there is no one besides you . . . for the* Lord *is a God who knows."* (1 Samuel 2:1-3)

Fast forward to the day a young virgin named Mary was told God's decision for her: She would become pregnant with the long-awaited Messiah. Mary had not been begging the Lord for a baby. She knew she would be ostracized and ridiculed for being pregnant out of wedlock; she could even be stoned. She was being handed a very, very hard assignment. But she also knew the heart of God, and that His decision was His best for her. So she didn't walk away. Instead, she said she was the Lord's servant and praised Him, believing He was in the business of knowing best.

> *My soul glorifies the Lord and my spirit rejoices in God my Savior . . . holy is his name.* (Luke 1:46-49)

God made decisions for each of these three women. Each experienced something they did not expect. Each was given a gift from God. Each had worries and concerns. (Think about how hard it would be to beg God for a child and then *give him up*!)

But most importantly, they had two very different responses to God's decisions for them. Eve became dissatisfied. She doubted God. But Hannah and Mary didn't dwell on their concerns. They focused on what they knew: their Lord. And they praised Him.

How about us? How do we handle God's decisions for our lives? Does it depend on the type of decision? Do we praise Him when it is a "yes" to what we've begged for, but grumble when He denies us something? Do we say, "I am your servant," and give Him glory when we get a shocking surprise? Or do we try to figure out how to fix it?

As mothers, can we say that our time spent in prayer and reading His Word has given us a profound intimacy with God that impacts how we respond? If He gives us a glimpse into His best for us and our children, do we know Him well enough to storm the gates of heaven with prayers for Him to bring forward something we know He has in store? Do we know His heart enough to gracefully and gratefully raise our hands in praise when He bestows something that is surely not a part of our plan—and accept that it is His?

Sisters, regardless of how God chooses to work through our lives, let's praise Him through it all.

"My heart rejoices in the Lord. My spirit rejoices in God my Savior."

His decision for us is good.

Prayer

Lord, as I think about this decision You have made for me, I say that it is Your right to make whatever decision You desire. And my heart rejoices in You. There is no one like You. You are amazing and glorious, and I choose to trust and believe that Your decision for me is best. Forgive me for the ways my fear sometimes gets in the way. I am Your servant. May it be to me as You have said. Amen.

Reflect

What decision has God made for your life that was a surprise? How can you rejoice in this decision? List three things about it for which you are grateful.

NOTES

Day 40

The Lord went ahead of them. He guided them during the day with a pillar of cloud, and he provided light at night with a pillar of fire. This allowed them to travel by day or by night. And the Lord did not remove the pillar of cloud or pillar of fire from its place in front of the people.

Exodus 13:21–22, NLT

Trust in Each Step of the Journey

Allison's son had trouble breathing since birth. Baby James was frequently in and out of the emergency room, subject to many medications, nebulizer treatments, and a lot of shrugged shoulders from the doctors. No one could figure out what was wrong. Until one day a biopsy came back positive for a rare genetic disease.

Allison and her husband, Chris, were shocked, but also strangely comforted by the fact that doctors finally knew what was wrong and could point them in the right direction.

They adjusted to their new normal, learning new techniques, ordering expensive equipment to keep his lungs clear, and resting in the fact that they were finally on a clear path—albeit one they never planned on traveling.

That is, until the phone rang a year later.

"We think there's been a mistake. The biopsy was compromised, and we're not sure James has that particular disease after all. We need to take a new biopsy. Do more tests."

Allison burst into tears. Could she handle suddenly being thrown back into the unknown and no longer knowing the path in front of her? The biopsy was taken and the waiting began. And continued for weeks. And months.

Six months later the doctor called. Allison answered the phone with a calmness that surprised even her. She heard the words she had dreaded: The original diagnosis was reversed, and they no longer knew what the malady was. Surprisingly, Allison was . . . okay.

In that waiting period, she had learned that God was the same yesterday as He is today and as He will be tomorrow. The direction of their journey may be different than what she was expecting, but the Lord was with them and would be guiding them. He knew where they were headed, even if they didn't. The day-by-day trusting had created a spiritual backbone and strength and knowledge in the Lord that wasn't there before.

Years later, once James's health stabilized, Allison and Chris began training for something they were passionate about: becoming a foster family. Almost immediately, they welcomed a four-year-old boy and a four-month-old baby girl. These children came from trauma, had multiple special needs, and brought challenges that drove Allison to her knees. But they were loved instantly and wove their way into their hearts in a way that felt permanent to her.

Yet the goal was to reunite the children with their biological parents, whom she genuinely loved and felt compassion for. Allison started wondering how this could end without multiple people getting their hearts broken. There were no answers on the horizon.

So, she had to wait . . . again. But this time, Allison felt different. As she put one foot in front of the other—each day, each week, each month—she trusted that God was leading them. There was no clear path forward, just the knowledge that He was going before them. And whatever the outcome, He would be there.

Oh, that didn't mean she didn't succumb to worry at times. Despite her best intentions, anxiety sometimes broke through when they had to go to court, or when last-minute changes were made by the social worker, or when important decisions kept getting delayed.

But there was also peace in the waiting. She felt her spiritual backbone support her. She realized that the experience with James had made her more courageous in her trust in the Lord. She realized that the God who knew the future allowed the waiting time with James to build her courage and trust for exactly this moment.

Eventually, after walking a long, rocky, tumultuous two-year path, Allison and Chris found themselves in the judge's chambers, holding up their hands in an oath to be the forever parents of these two precious children. And it was worth it. Every step.

Ladies, it is my prayer that as we learn how to find peace, we will also find purpose in our motherhood journey. The path can be long and winding. Sometimes it's wrought with pain or tears. But in our time together, I hope you have seen that there is far more beauty to be found. And courage. And meaning.

Let each trusting step forward be a prayer:

We know You.
We love You.
We trust You.
And with each step on the journey, Jesus, may we feel Your blessed peace.
Amen.

What Is Next for Your Journey of Peace?

Reflect

What are three important lessons that you have learned in this 40-day journey to find peace?

What is the one most important thing you want to do differently in the days and months to come to ensure that you experience His peace in all seasons of life?

Prayer

Lord, help me experience Your peace, and make me an instrument of Your peace, always. Amen.

The Prayer of St. Francis*

Lord, make me an instrument of Your peace:
where there is hatred, let me sow love;
where there is injury, pardon;
where there is doubt, faith;
where there is despair, hope;
where there is darkness, light;
where there is sadness, joy.

O divine Master, grant that I may not so much seek
to be consoled as to console,
to be understood as to understand,
to be loved as to love.
For it is in giving that we receive,
it is in pardoning that we are pardoned,
and it is in dying that we are born to eternal life.
Amen.

*Citation: Anonymous prayer, widely attributed to St. Francis of Assisi. First known publication: 1912 in a small French Catholic magazine, La Clochette (The Little Bell). http://www.franciscan-archive.org/franciscana/peace.html

Acknowledgments

Although books are attributed to a given author, they represent the hard work, dedication, and passion of dozens of people. This devotional is no different. To all those who worked on this: You have my deep thanks and admiration for the skills you bring to the table.

In particular, I'd like to thank the iDisciple team, especially David Henriksen, Kobus Johnsen, John Smith, Lianne Cornell, and Emma Lieblich, for their tremendous support and encouragement of the Find series, which is such a new and meaningful direction for me. A big thanks goes to my editor, Nancy Taylor, for her mad editing skills: taking my wordy pieces and crafting them to be just what the reader needs. I'm also very grateful to my friend Ashley Willis for being willing to write the Foreword.

This devo wouldn't exist without the dedication and insight of my senior editor, Katie Phillips, and the rest of our editorial/writing team. To Charlyn Elliot, my staff director; Lisa Rice; Beth Peazzoni; Tally Whitehead; Sue Birdseye; Brooke Turbyfill; and Bonnie Hauer: You are rock stars. I deeply appreciate your passion for this project, your willingness to draft up so many devotional stories, and your commitment to be moms who follow hard after God! A special thanks to the rest of my team for keeping everything running: Naomi Duncan, Eileen Kirkland, Theresa Colquitt, and especially Caroline Niziol, who came up with the idea for this devotional in the first place.

Finally, I'm incredibly grateful to our Heavenly Father—especially for giving me the people who made me a mom in the first place. To Jeff, Morgen, and Luke: You give me so much delight every day. This book is dedicated to you.